# Unbound

Heal from your past.

Reclaim your identity.

Unleash your potential.

Stefanie Libertore

Copyright © 2016 by Stefanie Libertore

*Unbound*
*Heal from your past. Reclaim your true identity. Unleash your potential.*
by Stefanie Libertore

Printed in the United States of America.

ISBN 9781498464376

All rights reserved solely by the author. The author guarantees all contents are original and do not infringe upon the legal rights of any other person or work. No part of this book may be reproduced in any form without the permission of the author. The views expressed in this book are not necessarily those of the publisher.

Unless otherwise indicated, Scripture quotations taken from the Amplified Bible (AMP). Copyright © 1954, 1958, 1962, 1964, 1965, 1987 by The Lockman Foundation. Used by permission. All rights reserved.

Scripture quotations taken from the New International Version (NIV). Copyright © 1973, 1978, 1984, 2011 by Biblica, Inc.™. Used by permission. All rights reserved.

Scripture quotations taken from the New King James Version (NKJV). Copyright © 1979, 1980, 1982 by Thomas Nelson, Inc. Used by permission. All rights reserved.

Scripture quotations taken from the New Living Translation (NLT). Copyright © 1996, 2004, 2007 by Tyndale House Foundation. Used by permission. All rights reserved.

Scripture quotations taken from The Message (MSG). Copyright © 1993, 1994, 1995, 1996, 2000, 2001, 2002. Used by permission of NavPress Publishing Group. Used by permission. All rights reserved.

www.xulonpress.com

# Dedication

To the only One who can ever make me complete—the Lover of my Soul, Jesus.
You came to me in the dirtiness of my choices, bound up my broken heart, proclaimed freedom to this captive,
and released me from the darkness of lies.
You. Make. Me. Glad.

Isaiah 61:1-8

# Table of Contents

| | |
|---|---|
| **Dedication** | v |
| Foreword | ix |
| Acknowledgements | xi |
| Endorsements | xiii |
| Introduction | xv |
| **Chapter 1**: *Good Mourning* | *21* |
| **Chapter 2**: *Reflections: Yours, Mine and the Truth* | *39* |
| **Chapter 3**: *Hearing from God* | *58* |
| **Chapter 4**: *Search & Rescue* | *75* |
| **Chapter 5**: *Masters of our Demise* | *91* |
| **Chapter 6**: *The Smoldering Embers of Anger* | *109* |
| **Chapter 7**: *Shedding the Grave Clothes of Shame* | 128 |
| **Chapter 8**: *Embracing Forgiveness* | 146 |
| **Chapter 9**: *Made for Intimacy* | 161 |
| **Chapter 10**: *He Loves Me, He Loves Me Knot* | 184 |
| **Chapter 11**: *Unchained Melody* | 201 |
| **Chapter 12**: *Unbound* | 214 |
| Endnotes | 225 |
| Resources | 229 |

# Foreword

The book you are holding is dangerous! Dangerous to the soul ties that hold hearts hostage. Dangerous to the status quo that lulls us to gloss over the ugly truth about the ways our souls have been shackled due to our sexual past...*or present*.

Stefanie Libertore in her brilliant debut book, **Unbound**, shares vulnerably about a topic that has been swept under the rugs of homes and churches across the world—SEX. Namely, our attitudes, experiences and wounds about sex.

**Unbound** shows how our past can fracture our present relationships—friendships, marriages, and parenting alike. It dares to speak the truth about shame, unforgiveness, and anger that wreak havoc on our emotional and spiritual health. Our world, joined by the Church, exhibits the results of sexual brokenness— hook-ups, divorce, porn, addictions, emotional and physical affairs, inability to commit, inability to be alone, promiscuity, and more.

We need a courageous and compassionate friend to help us *get real*, remove the Band-Aids from our soul-deep wounds, and get serious about our healing. A friend who has walked the journey and can point out both the pitfalls and the hidden beauty along the way. A friend who knows what freedom-fighting requires and is willing to coach us through it.

Stefanie Libertore is that friend! You will meet her in the pages of **Unbound** as she talks candidly about her journey toward healing from her own sexual past while leading her readers on an adventure with The Healer who transforms us.

Combined with creative exercises and object lessons from the author's own life, **Unbound** inspires us to believe we don't have to live cowering and captive by shame over our sexual past. We were created for life-giving relationships that bring honor and glory to God because He yearns for you and me to experience and understand the power, purpose, and beauty of sexuality by His design—in *holiness*.

Listen, this type of life transformation is worth fighting for. YOU are worth fighting for! But there *will* be a battle. Thankfully, you won't duke it out alone. Jesus stands ready and willing to take the lead as you step into the ring and take back what the enemy tried to steal. Seize the freedom and joy that has always been your birthright. **Unbound** is a training manual for spiritual warriors like YOU!

My prayer for you...

May the Lord guide your heart and mind as you experience and share the profound wisdom in this book. May today be the day you choose to begin a whole new chapter in YOUR life story: one that forever marks the turning point from shame, secrets, and regret to joy, transparency, and purpose! The chapter of your life entitled *Unbound!*

Freedom is gonna look great on you!
*Kim Dent, Founder*
*Dandelion Winds Ministry*
*\*Encourage \*Reconcile \*Love*
DandelionWinds.Com

# Acknowledgements

To my husband **Tony**, thank you for believing in me, encouraging me, and not being ashamed of my story. I love you. I'd say yes again, and again.

Profound thanks to **Jill Taylor, Mary Kay Wagner,** and **Fern Buzinski** for fanning the flame in me to write this book. You believed in me even before I did. Each of you light the path brilliantly for others.

Deepest gratitude to **Patricia Hoffman** for the constant flow of encouragement and prayers through the arduous process of writing this book. I value your wisdom, dear friend. Leading the pilot group with you left stretch marks! You are a living testimony of God's beautiful grace.

To my adventurous friend **Kim Dent**—thank you for your abundant encouragement during the writing process. Your joyful spirit is so crazy contagious. Thank you for being *safe*. You model Him so well.

To the staff of **Pregnancy Choices**, as well as friends at **High Mill Church of the Resurrection**—thank you for the many ways that you showed you were behind me all the way. Your words, cards, prayers, patience, gifts, and grace meant more than you'll ever know.

**Lonette Baity**, thank you for bringing **UNBOUND** to life in book form. You have amazing talent and vision. Thank you for reminding me that Christ's Bride wears combat boots. You be stylin' girl!

To **Rosemarie Hoover** (first edit) and **Linda Shaheen** (final edit), thank you for bringing excellence to this project.

To all the **broken and hurting women** who have invited (and who will) invite Christ into their stories and find Him faithful:

> You are brave.
> > You are beautiful.
> > > You are *Unbound*.

# Endorsements

In her new book, **UNBOUND**, Stefanie Libertore presents to us a Bible study built upon her experience and deep conviction that healing from one's sexual past is possible for every woman.

Stefanie has captured the Father's heart for purity and graciously invites us to enter in. Drawing upon story and Scripture, Stefanie skillfully dismantles the lies of seduction promoted by our culture. With bold expression and poignant insight into the heart longing to be set free, she shakes us to our very core and then skillfully brings us up from the depths to the truth that sets us free. With her many years as a teacher, leader, conference speaker, and writer, Stefanie takes us on a healing journey that leaves us courageously unbound.

Are you seeking to be challenged and changed in respect to your sexuality? This is a journey that will empower you to become the whole and healthy woman Christ designed you to be.
Fern Buzinski
Author, *Portraits: Unveiled Freedom*
*Hope for Healing After Abortion*

Audacious material straight from God's Word! This book, fresh from a brand new author, is written with compassion and tenderness from the heart of one who knows. Stefanie Libertore is authentic in building a relationship with the reader—she not only shares God's love but also helps the reader work through some amazingly difficult issues from the past and even perhaps from the present. **UNBOUND** has the power to set people free because it has the Source at its core. Amazingly great work—cudos to Ms. Libertore!
Jill Taylor, M.Ed.
Executive Director, Pregnancy Choices

With vulnerability, Stefanie Libertore takes the reader by the hand and leads her on a journey toward wholeness through a straight-forward, non-judgmental study. **UNBOUND** is a practical and lovingly confrontational study. I highly recommend this study to anyone who is struggling with a painful past.
Margaret Slabach
Author, *Threads of Hope*

*I came upon **UNBOUND** at a time when I was reeling from a past sin that I had a difficult time forgiving myself for. "I'm a Christian. I should have known better!" Throughout the pages of **UNBOUND** I found Truth, forgiveness, healing, and restoration. As God has shown His great love for me, I can now see more clearly that my story is really His story expressed through my life. This is a must do Bible study. You will come away with a renewed love for the Father as you feel His grace and mercy walk with you through healing!*
E. O.

*I was suicidal, emotionally paralyzed, and had sought out numerous professionals. When I finally turned to God and saw what He thinks about me and my past, my life changed! I am no longer suicidal, my marriage is thriving, and I now see me as God sees me. No amount of counseling has given me even a fraction of what God has healed in me. This study showed me the way to that healing.*
C. S.

*My heart was challenged by* **Unbound.** *I learned that God sees me through the blood-washed grace of Jesus! I have known His redemptive grace for years, but didn't really grab hold of His grace/hope until I worked through this study. God used* **Unbound** *to reach into my heart to places I thought were sealed up. It was as though I received a fresh spring cleaning! My garden is ripe and ready for harvest!*
R. N.

*Stefanie has a great gift of shining a new light on Scripture, which is one of the greatest highlights of her book. Watching the chains fall and women set free has been the greatest joy in facilitating a group through* **Unbound.** *Not one heart can remain unchanged after doing this study. He can rescue anyone from the deepest pit.*
L. B.

**Unbound** *wasn't written by an expert psychologist or a seasoned pastor. It is the heart cry of a woman who wrote from her personal experience and healing. It is covered with love and authenticity.*
B. C.

*This study gave me hope that I could be healed from my past. It always pointed me to Jesus, my only True Healer.*
J. D.

# Introduction

"*Pregnant? I can't be!*" *I whispered to myself.*
In hindsight, I shouldn't have been so surprised. After all, I'd been sexually active. I wasn't looking to get *pregnant*. I was looking for *love*.

Regrettably, and too easily, I ended the pregnancy in abortion.

I had no idea how my decision to abort would impact me for years to come. It shattered any healthy views that I had of myself. My self-worth sank to a miry depth, and self-hatred began to take root.

**This was not how I thought my life would turn out.**
   **This wasn't how my story was supposed to go…**

I felt betrayed by what I thought would fill my soul's void. I had come to believe the lies that love and acceptance were found in the arms of a man. Repeatedly, I tried to conform myself into *his* image instead of God's image.

The more I searched for "love," the emptier I felt inside. After several broken relationships, the intensity of those feelings grew deeper.
I felt *duped*.
   *Deceived.*
      *Cheated.*
         *Tricked.*

Hosea 2:7a described my longing heart:

**She will chase after her lovers but not catch them; she will look for them but not find them.**

My heart was hurt, empty, and broken. What remained of it became hardened. Trust became something that didn't come easily. I was angry and hurt. And out of my pain, I hurt others.

***Can you relate?***

Do you regret past choices?
> Are you still licking the wounds of your past hurts?
>> Does your marriage lack real joy and intimacy?
>>> Was your innocence robbed as a child? As a young adult?
>>>> Do you feel bound by your past? Broken beyond repair?

Every sexual choice we make affects us not only physically, but mentally, emotionally, and spiritually. Whether a longtime relationship or a one-night stand, we form soul ties with each sexual act, each sexual partner. Those ties leave an imprint on the soul that affects how we see ourselves, other people, sex, and even God. Often, we build walls around our hearts and make vows to self-protect. We lose trust in others, lose faith in God, and lose our sense of identity.

**It's the most ruthless kind of identity theft.**

God didn't leave me in that self-destructive state to search for love in vain. **LOVE** came after *me*. Love came and sought me out.

In 1991, I surrendered the shattered pieces of my heart to Christ and found forgiveness, *sweet forgiveness*. Not finished *in* me, a decade later, God began to bind up my wounds, heal my brokenness, and sever the ties of my sexual past.

In His wisdom, He allowed me to walk through the valley of my consequences in hopes that I would never return to that sin. His intent is that I –*and you*—would *"share in His holiness,"* as we allow His divine discipline to *"produce a harvest of righteousness and peace for those who have been trained by it"* (Hebrews 12:11).

And though God had done an enormous work of healing and restoration in my heart over many years, I still struggled with my view of men. I had a peculiar love/hate tug-of-war in my heart over them. I loved their attention, *needed* their approval, and wanted their love—all of which seemed to elude me. I had made men an idol and sacrificed my identity, my dignity, and my child at its altar.

Idolatry is having just a *wee bit* excessive attachment or devotion to something. We can make idols of just about anything.

Relationships.
> Marriage.
>> Children.
>>> Body image.
>>>> Even our own painful story can become an idol.

Giving Christ my story—the messy parts, the shameful parts, the needy parts, and the broken parts—elevated Him and brought my idols down.

**He can do the same for you.**
**He *wants* to do the same for you.**

You can trust God with your story. *All of it.*

Though you can't edit the painful chapters of your life, you *can* be at peace with Him and with your past. He has more than enough grace to cover your ugliest of chapters. The ending God promises is not full of butterfly wishes and fairy-tale kisses. Nor is it unrealistic like the dating shows that promise a happily-ever-after finale.

In His grace, you are part of *His*tory— God's grand finale of deliverance and restoration of a people who are dearly loved and called to be His very own.

## Introduction

Are you ready to let Him write His name on your heart? To craft His masterful story through the pages of your life?

**UNBOUND** is a Bible study that helps you find the freedom your soul longs for—freedom from the lies and ties of the past—helping to reclaim your true identity and unleash your amazing potential in Christ as a Freedom Fighter!

This book holds promise for you. The promise doesn't come from any of my words, or even my own story. It holds promise because there is a Promise-Keeper who has moved heaven and earth to reveal His love for you because He has promised to never leave you or abandon you.

There isn't a formula or magic prayer that will make your pain disappear. The peace and freedom you seek will take some effort on your part. It'll require facing tough memories, being honest with yourself, forgiving, and letting go so you can move on. Each chapter is topical and is intended to be worked through in a week by completing five different lessons. Move through the chapter one lesson at a time, giving yourself time to process it. **UNBOUND** is intended to be used within a small confidential group setting, but it can also be utilized individually or with a trusted pastor or counselor.

May I pray for you?

Lord, You know where she's come from. You know the pain she's endured and the questions in her heart. You know when she thought she would be swallowed up by the memories of events too painful to speak about. Lord, give this brave woman special grace for this journey. Thank You for promising to never leave her. Bring her to a place of peace. Heal her broken heart and her fractured identity. Make all things new for Your glory. In Jesus' Name. Amen.

Stefanie Libertore

# Chapter 1: Good Mourning

# Good Mourning

---∞---

*Day 1: God, Are You There?*

Seventeen years after my abortion, I was on an airplane headed for St. Petersburg, Russia. I had left my corporate marketing career for the mission field. After two years of going to India on short-term trips, I was set to begin a Discipleship Training School with Youth With A Mission (YWAM).

The YWAM base had started a pregnancy center ministry in the city. This could not be coincidental. I had served at a local pregnancy center 10 years earlier. And now here I was on an airplane with a post-abortion Bible study book in my carry-on bag to give to the base leaders on the other side of the world.

During the long flight I pulled out the book. My face flushed red hot as I began to see myself through its pages. I recognized the sin as my own and saw myself in the long list of symptoms of emotional and spiritual trauma. Heart racing, I quickly shut the book.

Nowhere to run.

    Nowhere to hide.

        And no parachute.

I felt as though a huge scab had been picked away and was bleeding uncontrollably, revealing an infected wound. For weeks afterward, I had a constant ache in my heart that wouldn't go away. I cried buckets of tears. I felt a deep, deep sense of grief.

One morning, I awoke early to have time with God before my classes started for the day. I pleaded with God to take away the pain I felt. I needed *rescued*. My heart hurt, and I didn't think I could take one more day of the pain. In my anguish, I refused to eat. I was prepared to go without food for as long as it took God to come to me and lift this heavy burden.

I was desperate.

I went to my class, dragging my burden with me. When I came home that evening, I returned to prayer and Bible reading. I felt God leading me to read Nehemiah 8. Verse 10 was my breakthrough:

> Then he said to them, *"Go and enjoy choice food and sweet drink...This day is holy to our LORD. Do not grieve, for the joy of the LORD is your strength."*

In my heart, I understood God saying to me, *"Stefanie, this is a holy day to Me. This day is cause for celebration, so eat! I've been waiting for this day for many years. I've been waiting for your awakening—your breakthrough! My delight and joy is in you and **I** will be your strength through these next days."*

When I returned to the United States six months later, I made a call to the local pregnancy center where I had formerly volunteered. Now I was a client. I was put in touch with the post-abortion recovery facilitator and attended a 12-week Bible study to heal from that ginormous wound in my life.

For years afterward, I had wondered why God chose to send me to Russia in order to "do business" with me. How ironic that He brought me to the bitter cold of Russia to *thaw* me out emotionally.

I had begged God to "lift my burden." He certainly did, but it didn't happen overnight. In fact, He is still healing and restoring me.

How about you?

Did life take you down a road that you didn't expect? Have you cried yourself to sleep wondering, *"This isn't how I thought my life would turn out?"* Perhaps you've experienced something so painful, so messy, that you've even questioned God's love and goodness.

You're not alone.

We can't change our story, but God can cause us to be at peace with our past no matter how broken it's left us. You may not see it yet, but it's there. HOPE.

As we set out on our journey, we're going to start by looking at grief. Not exactly the "hopeful" start you were looking for? Believe me, it's exactly where we need to be whether we realize it or not. Grief is like a pool in which we've been wading in chest high. For some, the swells of grief have consumed us, and we feel as though we are drowning. It's in this place of sorrow that we will find our Comforter if we invite Him into our story.

The story of Lazarus in John 11 reveals a story of hope in the midst of death, deep grief, and disappointment. It's a story that I can relate to because I've experienced loss. Something tells me that you have, too.

**Let's pray**: *God, I'm stuck in my hurt, and sometimes I can't see You through my tears. Awaken hope in me and bring me to a place of peace. In Jesus' Name. Amen.*

**Read John 11:1-45.**

Lazarus, the brother of the legendary sisters, Mary and Martha, was sick. He was *really* sick. So the sisters sent word to Jesus saying, *"Lord, he whom you love is ill"* (vs. 11:3). They were probably confident that Jesus would come. They were friends. They were *close*. After sending word to Jesus, maybe they didn't allow themselves to grow overly concerned over Lazarus' worsening condition. After all, *Jesus would come.*

***Now Jesus loved Martha and her sister and Lazarus. So when he heard that Lazarus was sick, he stayed where he was two more days. (John 11:5-6)***

Jesus gets the message to hurry to Bethany, but surprisingly He doesn't budge. In fact, Jesus stays put for another two days. Lazarus' condition takes a dive and with it, Mary and Martha's confidence in Jesus' love.

His no-show leaves them wondering.
    Questioning.
  Doubting.

You too? When that abuse happened, or that betrayal hit you out of nowhere—did you, like Mary and Martha, wonder what Jesus was doing? Where He was in it all? Why He took so long to show up?

***Finally, he said to his disciples, "Let's go back to Judea." But his disciples objected. (John 11:7-8 NLT)***

The disciples objected because there was danger in Judea. The Jews had tried to stone Jesus and now He wants to go back? Jesus never cowered in fear. He wasn't afraid to face dangerous situations to rescue those in darkness.

Like those early followers, we often object to the places Jesus wants to take us on our healing journey. Going back can't be the way to freedom. Or can it?

**What objections (or doubts) do you have as you begin this journey of healing from your past?**

**Write out John 11:14-15.**

In this chapter, Jesus uses the word *believe* six times. The repetition of the word is meant to grab our attention. **What do you think the Lord may be asking you to believe about your sexual past? About your future?**

*When Martha heard that Jesus was coming, she went out to meet him, but Mary stayed at home.*
*(John 11:20)*

When we hurt, we can sometimes go through the motions of daily routines, fluctuating between denial and despondency. I imagine Mary and Martha experienced many emotions, thoughts, and accusations in those first four days as they questioned, wondered, doubted, and fought back the ebb and flow of their anger about Jesus' absence. Like them, our unanswered questions can cause us to doubt what we thought we knew. We check out emotionally, putting up walls of self-protection.

Maybe that's why Mary *stayed at home* while Martha went to meet with Jesus. The ESV says, *"...but Mary remained seated."*

Now I can't possibly know what was going through Mary's mind when she heard that Jesus had finally come. But here's one way that we can look at it: It's like a football game between rival teams. It's the 4th quarter, and the score is tied. Your team has the ball at the 5-yard line with just seconds remaining. The noise level in the stadium is deafening. All eyes are on the field. The ball snaps, and everyone is out of their seats.

That is, all except Mary. *She remains seated.*

Our unresolved pain can lead us to question God's goodness, and we're *unmoved*. We stop believing that He can help. Instead, we believe the lie that He doesn't want to. As Martha came with her question, we come casting judgment with ours, *"Lord, if You had been here..."*

**God is unafraid of your questions. Fill in your "if only" statement:**

"Lord, if You had been here, _____
_____."

"Lord, if You had been here, I wouldn't have died inside when _____
_____."

God is unafraid of your questions and doubts. He is moved with compassion for you even if you are unmoved toward Him.

 **My "I Get It!" thought for today:**

## Good Mourning

### Day 2: Moving Stones

We've all heard the saying, "Hindsight is 20/20." In other words, it's only after we come through the circumstance at hand that we can see it clearly—making any sense of it.

As someone whose vision is pathetically dim without the assistance of contact lenses or glasses, this is a notion that I warmly embrace. Except sometimes, as hard as we may try, seeing 20/20 in those dark places of our lives can be virtually impossible. We must trust El Roi—*The God who Sees*—and rest in His heart of goodness toward us, believing that He will cause all things to work for the good of those that love Him (Romans 8:28).

In John 11, Mary, Martha, and Jesus' disciples needed fresh eyes of faith to receive what Jesus was about to do.

Let's ask God to open our eyes:

> *Father, help me to see Your bigger picture. You've brought me through more than I thought I could come through. Give me fresh eyes of faith to trust Your heart toward me and to let go of those things that cannot be changed. In Jesus' Name, Amen.*

**Read John 11: 1-45.**

> ***Jesus said to her, "I am the resurrection and the life. He who believes in me will live, even though he dies; and whoever lives and believes in me will never die. Do you believe this? (John 11:25-26)***

Did you notice how Jesus introduced Himself? To the woman at the well, He revealed Himself as Living Water. To those who were hungry on the hillside, He was The Bread of Heaven. And now, to a grieving sister, Jesus reveals Himself as The Resurrection and the Life.

Jesus asks, *"Do you believe this?"*

When asking my daughter a question, (particularly when she's watching TV), she has been known to respond with, *"Wait. What?"* However simple the question, the sound of my voice can usually shake her out of the TV-zone and into the here-and-now. Like my daughter, maybe Martha shook her head as if to clear it for better reception. *"Wait. What did He just say?"* Jesus' question forces us out of our despondency and back to the here-and-now.

Jesus asks us the same question He asked Mary long ago, ***"Do you believe this?"***

**What in your life needs resurrected?**


> ***She called Mary aside from the mourners and told her, "The Teacher is here and wants to see you." Now Jesus had not yet entered the village, but was still at the place where Martha had met him. (John 11:28, 30 NLT)***

Scripture points out that Jesus did not enter the village but stayed at the place where Martha met him. I believe that Jesus does not go anywhere He's not been invited. He possesses the power to heal and restore, but He wants to be invited into the process.

Several years ago, I injured my shoulder. One wrong movement and I experienced hot searing pain that would bring me to tears. It was awful. I suffered with the pain for two years. I never sought out a doctor for help. Don't ask me why. I came to accept my limitations of movement as my "new normal."

But one Sunday morning at church, our pastor called for those who needed healing to come to the front of the sanctuary for prayer. This was not a common practice at our church. I went *swiftly*. I was in so much pain that it *motivated* me into action. I needed relief. When he prayed for me, my arm felt warm, then hot, but not in a bad way. Back at my seat, I began to move my arm around in ways that I normally couldn't. God had healed my shoulder.

No. More. Pain.

**Are you desperate for God to heal your heart? Will you invite Him into your situation? Into your story? He can restore you. He *wants* to restore you.**

When Mary meets Jesus, not surprisingly, she brings the same question (or accusation) that her sister Martha did: *"Jesus, if only you had been here...."*

Those that surrounded Mary and Martha also came with their blazing accusations: *"He healed others, couldn't He have kept Lazarus from dying?"*

Our sincere questions can be the spark that sets the whole forest ablaze with doubt and mistrust in God. And even in our profound healing, there may be those who will question where God was in our ordeal—wondering why we even had to experience heartbreak or pain in the first place.

*When Jesus saw her weeping, and the Jews who had come along with her also weeping, he was deeply moved in spirit and troubled...Jesus wept. (John 11:33, 35)*

**Write out John 11:34-35.**

Did you catch that? It's the invitation. Mary, Martha, and the mourners invited Jesus into their grief. And what was Jesus' response?

*He wept.*

Jesus wept. He grieves over your pain, your abuse, and your choices that produced brokenness.

**How does it feel to know that Jesus wept at Lazarus' tomb? Do you believe He cries over every injustice that you've experienced?**

And then Jesus did something unthinkable.

> *"Take away the stone," He said. "But Lord," said Martha, the sister of the dead man, "by this time there is a bad odor, for he has been there four days." (John 11:39)*

**Read John 11:39 and note how many days Lazarus had been dead:** _____

We can only imagine the commotion among the crowd at His command. Lazarus had been dead for four days. By that time, the body was severely decayed. But to see the miracle, the obstacle (the stone) needed to be removed.

Once again, Martha objected. How can exposing death be the answer?

In order to experience our own resurrection, we need to remove the obstacles that are keeping us from the abundant life in Christ that He promises all Believers. Like Martha, we may object to exposing the decay of our choices or the pain of a wound inflicted upon us. But it was only in exposing Lazarus' true condition that Jesus' power was made manifest.

> *...He cried out in a loud voice, "Lazarus, come out." The man who had died came out, his hands and feet bound with linen strips, and his face wrapped with a cloth. Jesus said to them, "Unbind him, and let him go." (John 11:43-44 ESV)*

You know how this story ends. The invitation to bring Jesus into the situation—into their grief and loss—*moved* Jesus to action.

And a **dead man** came to life.

What He did for Lazarus He will do for you. He can resurrect a dead heart or a dead marriage. He can bring life—*vibrant life*—to decaying views you may have about yourself, men, sex, and God.

**Do you believe?**

 My "I Get It!" thought for today:

## Good Mourning

### Day 3: The Uneasiness of Grief

We've seen through the story of Lazarus and my own shared story that we experience grief through loss. It can be loss at the hand of another, through our own choices, or something totally out of our control. No matter how you slice it, grief is the result of loss. It can vary in intensity, and it can be overwhelming to our hearts. Author John Eldredge says it well, *"Grief is a form of validation; it says the wound mattered. It mattered. You mattered. That's not the way life was supposed to go."*

Sometimes we get flat lined in our emotions because grief has consumed us. We've been stuck for so long in our pain that we don't even realize our reduced ability to express emotions. We are *numb*.

A Biblical definition of grief can mean *to make one uneasy*. As already stated, grief is a natural reaction to loss. God knows your pain. He knows your grief. And He knows how you are made. Grief *makes one uneasy* so that you won't stay there. God's desire is to see you move through the valley of grief and into acceptance and healing.

> **Let's pray:** *Father, I admit I feel "uneasy" in my soul, but it's hard to see what makes me feel that way. Put Your divine finger on those roots so that I can see it, call it what it is, and move past it victoriously. In Jesus' Name. Amen.*

Sometimes we hurt and don't know why. In order to move beyond our grief, we need to be able to name it – call it what it is – **loss**. If we don't identify the roots of our pain, it will leave us feeling confused and "stuck." Worst of all, it can leave us feeling hopeless.

**What have you lost as a result of your sexual past? (Innocence, trust, self-esteem, etc.)**

**Read Joel 2:25 in the following versions below:**

> *"And I will **restore** to you the years that the locust hath eaten, the cankerworm, and the caterpillar, and the palmerworm, my great army which I sent among you."* (KJV)

> *"I will **repay** you for the years the locusts have eaten – the great locust and the young locust, the other locusts and the locust swarm – my great army that I sent among you."* (NIV)

**Do you think there is a difference between restore and repay? Explain.**

We can't resurrect a loved one who has died. In the same way, there are things we've lost that can't be replaced. However, there is much that God can **restore** when we say "yes" to Him. A friend opened up this verse to me in the Hebrew language, and it greatly impacted me:

The word *restore* in the Hebrew is *shalam*, and it can mean *to cause to be at peace*.

Let's define a few more words, and then we'll tie it together at the end:

- Cankerworm: Hebrew *yeleq* (yel' lek) which means *to lick up*
- Caterpillar: Hebrew *chaciyl* (khä·sēl') which means *to devour*
- Palmerworm: Hebrew *gazam* (gä·zäm') which means *to pull in pieces/pluck off*

When we grieve in unhealthy ways, it can reveal that we've been *licking* our wounds. Too much licking keeps the wound open, unable to heal. One who licks her wounds is someone who excessively focuses on her pain and never seems to heal from it. When we bring our hurts to God instead of dwelling on them alone, we look back at our pasts so that we can move *forward*.

The grief of our losses mixed with a toxic combination of guilt and shame from our sexual past can be like choice morsels that go down into the inmost parts of our being, *devouring* our thoughts, attitudes, sleep, trust, and peace. Like a cancer, it worms its way in to ravage our true identities – *pulling to pieces* any dignity, honor, or hope.

I licked my abortion wound for 17 years until I began to see it the way that God did. After that wound was healed, I was able to examine my sexual past and begin the long healing process of grieving my losses and moving on. Restoration is a life-long process.

**What is the incident(s) in your sexual past that you are having a hard time getting past?**


**How have you been licking the wounds from your past?**


**In what ways has your sexual past devoured you or pulled you to pieces?**


**Reread Joel 2:25 and write it out.**


**Write the Hebrew meaning of the word restore:**


Now let's tie all of this together. A little history of the locust banquet in the book of Joel reveals that God sent the locusts to His people with the intent that they would turn from their sin and come back to Him. And though His people faced devastation and great loss due to their sin, God was in essence saying:

*"I (God) will cause you to be at peace with the years that the locusts have eaten – the years of licking your wounds; the years that have been devoured; the years that you felt pulled to pieces..."*

**Do you believe that God can cause you to be at peace with your past? Why or why not?**


Come to God with your questions. Allow the Spirit of God to access those hidden corners of your heart. He is faithful and committed to your healing. And He is able to do the unimaginable: to cause you to be at peace with your past and with yourself.

 **My "I Get It!" thought for today:**

## Good Mourning

### *Day 4: Lifting the Mask of Grief*

Losses cause us to grieve. When we're faced with pain, we often jump into action to get our minds off the pain that's threatening us. We stay busy. We drink. We raid the refrigerator. These are called coping mechanisms, and they are the things (or people) we run to for comfort. Our attempts to comfort ourselves fall so short of the comfort that awaits us from the Comforter Himself. I understand why we do it though: we're afraid of coming undone or unraveled. But what we don't see is that our cocoon of coping is actually hurting us more than it is helping us.

In one of my healing groups, I presented the women with their own butterfly cocoon. The species of butterfly was known as a *Question Mark* for its unique markings. I had no idea how appropriate it would turn out to be. Each of these beautiful women had come with their own questions.

Questions about a painful past.
    Questions about a hopeful future.

I explained that the butterflies would hatch in a few days. The cocoon would turn from its current shade of gray to black before it hatched. After hatching, the butterfly would be ready to fly in 24 hours after its wings were dry. However, by God's design, one of the butterflies had hatched just before our group had gathered. As I observed the newly born creature, I noticed a single drop of blood on the bottom of the box. Oh, the mercy of our God! Breaking free from that tight cocoon is hard work. Birth is difficult. Hard. Messy.

The butterfly had wiggled and wrestled until it broke through its cocoon. We wiggle and wrestle in our discomfort, don't we? Our once-safe cocoon has now become a liability. We need a breakthrough. Like the butterfly cocoon, things are darkest just before our breakthrough comes. And the blood? A glorious reminder that our freedom came at a cost: Jesus' blood for our freedom, our healing.

Each woman returned the following week with her own special hatching story. It was a turning point of sorts for each of them. I could only marvel at God's wisdom and ability to speak to each heart through the birth of a tiny winged creature.

*Real* living happens when our cocoons of coping become unraveled and we break free from its hold. Remember the Biblical definition of grief? (Grief can mean *to make one uneasy*.) We are not meant to stay in that place of unease, merely coping, limping along in life and in our relationships. Instead, we are meant to move through the valley of grief into a place of peace or acceptance.

Today we're going to explore *how* we've been coping or covering up our hurts. Let's look at the definition of cope:

---

**Merriam-Webster Dictionary**
**Cope:** *something that conceals or covers*
Synonyms: mask, veil

---

According to this definition, coping is concealing or covering grief under a mask. Anything but authentic.

**Following is a list of unhealthy ways we may be masking grief. Circle the ones that apply to you and write in the "triggers" that cause you to react in those ways.**

| Methods of Coping | Situational/Emotional Triggers |
|---|---|
| Alcohol | |
| Anger/Rage | |
| Berate/Nag | |
| Clothing choices (to hide or seek attention) | |
| Computer Games | |
| Control | |
| Drugs (legal/illegal) | |
| Eating Disorders | |
| Emotional Affairs/Fantasizing | |
| Emotionally Withdraw/Isolate | |
| Gossiping | |
| Hypercritical | |
| Internet/Chat Rooms/Email | |
| Over-commitment to Work/Church Service | |
| Perfectionism | |
| Sexual Affair/Promiscuity | |
| Shopping/Spending | |
| Smoking | |
| Television | |
| Too Much Time on Phone | |
| Weight Gain | |
| Other: | |

Some methods of coping are obvious, like smoking, using drugs or alcohol. Let's be honest: alcohol or drugs are artificial quick fixes that postpone the inevitable and only add to your problems. If you think you have a problem and can't quit on your own, call *Alcoholics Anonymous* or *Narcotics Anonymous* and get some help.

From the book **CAPTIVATING: UNVEILING THE MYSTERY OF A WOMAN'S SOUL**, authors John and Stasi Eldredge say,

> *"[The ways in which we choose to cope can] entangle themselves in our souls like a cancer and, once attached, become addictions that are both cruel and relentless. Though we seek them out for a little relief from the sorrows of life, addictions turn on us and imprison us in chains that separate us from the heart of God and others as well. It is a lonely prison of our own making, each chain forged in the fire of our indulgent choice."*

Less obvious (and more socially acceptable) methods of coping can be over-commitment to work or service to church. Masks that come with a feel-good pat on the back can be the hardest to uncover.

God does not want us to **cope**. He wants us to **overcome**. We can do that only with His help. Let's start with an honest confession:

*God, You know me better than I know myself. Show me the masks I've been hiding behind. Open my eyes and my heart to understand what triggers this behavior and help me to overcome by Your power. In Jesus' Name. Amen.*

**Review the chart of coping methods. In what ways have you been coping? Were you surprised by any of your findings?**

Let's get honest. What is driving our need to cope? What masks are we hiding behind? What are we *longing* for? What is our soul *craving*? In *what* are we seeking comfort? We must stop looking to other people or other means to cope with our pain. Before indulging, stop and ask yourself, "When have I felt this way before and why? Will what I'm about to do actually scratch my itch, or will it only make it worse?"

**Read Jeremiah 2:12-13 (MSG)**
*"Stand in shock, heavens, at what you see!*
*Throw up your hands in disbelief—this can't be!" God's Decree.*
*"My people have committed a compound sin:*
*they've walked out on me, the fountain*
*Of fresh flowing waters, and then dug cisterns—*
*cisterns that leak, cisterns that are no better than sieves.*

A cistern is an artificial reservoir for holding liquids. The Bible mentions cisterns many times because they were a means of collecting rainwater in an otherwise very dry climate. In addition, they came to be regarded as a measure of security.

**Look up the definition of ARTIFICIAL and write it out below.**

**How does Jeremiah 2:12-13 relate to unhealthy methods of coping?**

**Write out the following verses and note how we should respond to God, the Fountain of Flowing Waters.**

**James 4:7-10**

**Jeremiah 31:19**

**I John 1:9**

God responds to our humility and will surely lift us up when we admit our neediness. Go ahead and lift that mask and let the Sonshine warm your face.

**Write out Psalm 31:16 and conclude your homework with a prayer to God.**

 My "I Get It!" thought for today:

# Good Mourning

## Day 5: Good Mourning

In our study this week on grief, we've looked at the ways we've been coping with grief, as well as how it has impacted our relationships vertically (with God) and horizontally (with others). Through your journey thus far, I hope you have been able to connect the dots between past hurts and present hang-ups. Masking our pain doesn't make it go away. Stuffing our hurts denies God's power to heal.

So how do we practically cause our bitter tears to bring us to a place of peace?

In Deuteronomy 30:19-20, Moses challenged the Israelites, *"This day I call the heavens and the earth as witnesses against you that I have set before you life and death, blessings and curses. Now choose life, so that you and your children may live and that you may love the LORD your God, listen, to his voice, and hold fast to him. For the LORD is your life..."*

God doesn't force His will on anyone. He lets us decide whether to follow Him or reject Him. This decision, however, is a life-or-death matter. God wants us to realize this, for He would like us all to choose life. Daily, in each new situation, we must affirm and reinforce this commitment.

> **Let's pray:** *God, I am weak. Coping has left me only empty and wanting. Worse of all, I hurt more because I know what I'm doing leads to death. Death in my relationships. Death of my true identity. Death in ways I don't even realize. I want to choose life in every situation I face. Help me in my weakness to choose life. In Jesus' Name. Amen.*

What prompts unhealthy methods of coping is our denial of pain. We wrongly convince ourselves that we can handle it. "No big deal. I'm strong." But God wants us to forsake our cisterns – those artificial ways of dealing with things that only lead to more brokenness. His invitation is that you CHOOSE LIFE in your daily, moment-by-moment living.

When you are lonely, *choose life*!
When you feel hurt, *choose life*!
When you are angry, *choose life*!
When you are stressed out, *choose life*!
When you have bad memories, *choose life*!
When you feel ashamed, *choose life*!
When you feel disrespected, *choose life*!
When you need to feel in control, *choose life*!

God would never tell us to do something unless it was in our power to choose it. We *can* overcome. But what does that look like in real life?

Following are some healthy responses to pain, hurt, grief, and sadness.

| Pray | Prayer brings God into your situation. Talk and listen to God. |
|---|---|
| Meditate on God's Word | God's Word centers our thoughts. It offers comfort, answers to questions, exposes lies, wrong attitudes, and more. |
| Journal | Turn your thoughts into letters to God. Journaling can be very therapeutic in helping to release negative emotions and discover hidden ones. |
| Go for a walk/exercise | Exercise relieves stress, provides an emotional lift, promotes better sleep, and more. |
| Read a good book | Read about real people and how they overcame obstacles in their life. (Beware of books with provocative themes that could do more harm than good.) |
| Tap into your creative side | Paint, draw, write, sculpt, craft! |

Writing about painful experiences can be one key to successful recovery. I have used all of the above-mentioned methods to work through my own painful emotions. The Psalms offer beautiful examples of expressions of grief and the hope that comes as one clings to God and His infallible Truth.

**Read Psalm 13.**

Written by David, the theme of this psalm is praying for relief from despair. Throughout many psalms, David often claimed that God was slow to act on his behalf. David found freedom and strength in expressing his feelings to God. By the end of his prayer, he was able to profess hope in God and trusted in His timing and deliverance.

Tap into your creative side and write your own psalm or poem to God. Read Psalm 13 again in several different versions. Think about what David might have been facing in his life. Think of the emotions he may have experienced. How does your story relate to his? Who are your enemies? *What* are your enemies? Use this psalm to express your own pain, questions, and hope to God.

*My Personal Psalm...*

**My "I Get It!" thought for today:**

Chapter 2:
Reflections: Yours, Mine & the Truth

# Reflections: Yours, Mine & the Truth

### Day 1: Up From the Dirt

My first memory of any kind of encounter with God happened at the tender age of seven. My parents divorced when I was three years old. In the middle of first grade, we moved across town and into the projects. Under roof were my mother, grandmother, two older sisters, and me.

On a warm summer day, I found a stick and began digging in the dirt in the courtyard. During my excavation, I unearthed a crucifix. Suddenly I was a pirate who had found treasure. I buried it and dug it up over and over again. I don't remember how many times I did that. The last time I dug it up, something happened that still makes my jaw drop open decades later. As I brought up the crucifix from the dirt, I noticed that the Jesus figure was gone; only the crucifix remained. I dug in places I hadn't dug before. I searched everywhere for Him. Jesus was *gone!*

I sat there looking down at the cross in my dirty little hand. I was perplexed. Stunned. *Where did He go?* I wondered.

I would think about that incident numerous times over the next 19 years until I finally understood what He wanted to reveal to me about Himself.

Fast forward to September 26, 1991. I was 25 years old. That was the day I made a choice to trade my despair for joy and stumbled through a prayer to ask Jesus to become my All in all. I really didn't know what that would mean in the long-term, but in faith, I believed He could make the difference I needed.

It wasn't long after that sweet day in September when God brought the memory to mind of a little girl finding "treasure" in the dirt. I wondered again, as I'd done hundreds of times since that summer day in 1973—*where did Jesus go?* In a flash of understanding, God finally answered my question.

*"I'm alive, Stefanie. I'm not on the cross, and I'm not in the grave. I'm ALIVE!"*

He came to me in the dirt when I was seven years old. That was long before I knew I needed a Savior—long before I took paths far from Him.

*So* long before...

Those years in between were filled with mistrust, grief, and uncertainty. I had plenty of good times too, but I remember more clouds than sunshine during that time. My unplanned pregnancy and abortion at age 18 led to my unraveling. My search for significance led me into many relationships that ended before they started. My heart became increasingly hardened as I swallowed more rejection and abandonment. Emotionally, I was on a downward spiral and falling fast.

And that's when He came to me in the dirt **again**. Only this time, I wasn't a child. I was a 25-year-old woman, and I was stuck in the dirtiness of my choices.

Then in 2002, God began to heal my brokenness, and I found forgiveness and peace for the abortion that nearly devastated me. Since that time, He has been intricately involved in my healing process—removing scabs, scar tissue, and memories. He's brought an enormous amount of healing to my sexual past through various Bible studies, as well as the writing of this book. Over many years, God has been actively reconstructing my views of myself, men, sex, and what I believe about God Himself.

In order to re-construct something rightly, the old foundation has to go. All the old junk has to be torn down and thrown out. All the lies, all the wrong thinking—it *all* has to go. Jesus wasn't afraid to meet me in my dirt. And He isn't afraid to meet you in yours. He'll meet you right where you are and lift you out.

And that's why you're here. The next weeks are about tearing down the old lies and reconstructing with the Truth so that He can establish you into an oak of righteousness that the Lord has planted for His own glory (Isaiah 61:3). Why? Because He has work for you to do!

**Write out Isaiah 61:1-3 and underline what Jesus came to do for you:**

**Now write out verse 4:**

**Who is "they" referring to?**

**Do one more thing for yourself. Rewrite Isaiah 61:4 inserting your own name in place of "they."**

Your healing is important not only to yourself, but to others. There's someone out there who will need the hope you'll give her!

He's ready, able, and willing to do this in your life.

 **My "I Get It!" thought for today is:**

# Reflections: Yours, Mine & the Truth

## *Day 2: Mirror, Mirror on the Wall...*

Over the course of this study, we will expose what we've come to believe about ourselves, others, sex, and God. Due to brokenness and wounding in our lives, our perception of ourselves has become tangled and twisted. *We hide.* We hide in the dark of fear and brokenness. Hiding *seems* safe. But the shadows are the secret places of shame, and they rob us of peace. The Light beckons us to come—not to expose our insecurities and weakness, but to destroy the power of darkness and bring us into the safety of God's embrace.

God will cover you with His righteous covering. He will never leave you naked and ashamed because He promises that *"those who look to him are radiant, their faces are never covered with shame"* (Psalm 34:5 NIV).

**Let's pray:**

> *Lord, shine the light of Your truth on how I see You and how I see myself. Divide truth and lies. Give me courage to face the things You show me and the power through the Holy Spirit to overcome them. In Jesus' Name. Amen.*

Imagine walking into a large room filled with mirrors. The room is warmly lit—not dark, but dim. There are dozens upon dozens of mirrors lining the walls. Many more are set up on easels. There are vintage mirrors with ornate frames, and others are simple and rather plain. There are small mirrors and large mirrors, rectangular and oval mirrors. You can't help but catch your reflection as you look around the room. You look up, and the ceiling is covered with one huge mirror. You feel as if you're on display. You look away, but you catch a glimpse of your image from every angle. You almost feel the room closing in on you.

And then you notice a mirror you hadn't spotted before.

It's broken. *Shattered*—although it's still intact within the frame. It looks as though someone had flung her well-heeled shoe at it and hit her mark. You knit your brow, wondering what could cause such a reaction. The temptation to reach out and touch your reflection overtakes you. You touch the mirror. Then slowly you reach your hand to your face, assuring yourself that you are not as broken as what your image reflects. Finally, you pull yourself away. To your right you notice a funhouse mirror. You look short and stout, and you giggle as you remember summer days of long ago at the fair with friends. You make funny faces just as you used to when you were 10 years old. You move from side to side and make silly motions with your arms and hands. You know that what you see reflected is not reality, but you feel a cloud darken your soul. Your smile fades. You finally walk away.

**In the space below, write down any thoughts and feelings you had while you walked through that descriptive mirrored room.**



**Which mirror do you relate to the most: the shattered mirror or the funhouse mirror? Why?**

**If you were standing in front of a mirror with Jesus looking over your shoulder, what would He say about you?**

**What did you discover about your view of yourself that you did not realize before?**

Mirrors. Maybe you dread them, maybe you don't. Many of us would rather avoid them altogether. Oh, we'll look long enough to apply the make-up and make ourselves presentable for the day, but we don't really *see* ourselves. That might risk exposure. I think if we're honest, many would say that they *hide*.

**Read Genesis 3:1-11. What emotion did Adam and Eve feel after eating the forbidden fruit, and what was their course of action? (vs. 7)**

**Why were Adam and Eve afraid? (vs. 10)**

**Write out God's response in verse 11a:**

**Who told *you* that you were naked?**

Satan, a cunning opportunist, will step in at the best and worst of times and whisper lies into our soul. Unless we shut him up with **God's** truth right away, his lies will wreak havoc on us. Lies can escape the lips of those we trust like family, friends, or a spouse. And because we trust and love them, words spoken in anger or with manipulation become seeds of self-doubt and shame that can take root in our hearts.

Those messages, spoken over and over, can become truth that we adopt. If we listen or entertain those lies, the enemy of your soul will tell you who you are. You'll question your worth, your value, your importance. Your view of yourself will become warped like a funhouse mirror. Your trust in others? Shattered. And your view of God? That gets distorted too.

## ACTIVITY

> Today you will begin an activity that should be finished by the end of the week. Give yourself a one-hour time limit so that you don't overthink it. Here's what you will do:
>
> On a piece of poster board, create a "View-of-Yourself Collage." You are not drawing or using an actual picture of yourself for this project. Instead, you will use words or images from a magazine that will describe/articulate your view of yourself as a result of your sexual past.
>
> If you're doing this study with others, be prepared to share your collage with the group.

*Lord, help me resist the urge to hide my hurt, pain, and shame from You. My deepest scars are not hidden from You. Bring them to the surface of my heart so they can be illuminated by the Light of your Love. Re-frame my view of myself so that my image mirrors Yours in every area of my life. In Jesus' Name. Amen.*

 **My "I Get It!" thought for today is:**

### Reflections: Yours, Mine & the Truth

*Day 3: Who's the Fairest One of All?*

For the next two days, we're going to "hunker down" and explore God's character. The term "hunker down" can mean *to kneel down*. What an appropriate position for us to take as we look afresh into the vastness of our God. He's more than we'll be able to glean in a couple days' time, but we'll learn enough to know that He is *amazing* and One worth reflecting. My hope is that we'll discover the false images we have of God and ourselves and allow God to rebuild and restore us into *His* image.

If you're physically able, *hunker down* or kneel to pray:

> *Lord, open my eyes to see how wonderful You are. Give me a fresh vision of Your greatness. I believe You are who You say You are and that nothing is impossible for You. Change me from the inside out. In Jesus' Name. Amen.*

Our view of God is formed early in our life. It's formed by the people around us and their views of God, spoken and unspoken. Our church background also influences our view of God, regardless of denomination. If God was misrepresented, we may have grown fearful of Him in the *wrong* sense of the word—anticipating His displeasure on any given day. And if we've missed the mark (which all of us have), we will tend to stay at a distance from Him.

**Who influenced your views of God (positively or negatively)?**

**Think of at least three things (right or wrong) that you learned about God as a child.**

**As a child, did you like God? Why or why not?**

**Did your views of God change as you grew into adolescence and adulthood? If so, how?**

It's very difficult to separate our view of God from our view of our earthly father. For example, if our dad was distant, harsh, abusive, critical, or demanding, chances are we probably view God much the same way.
Below, briefly describe your father and mother.

| Describe your FATHER using 10 adjectives | Describe your MOTHER using 10 adjectives |
|---|---|
|  |  |
|  |  |
|  |  |
|  |  |
|  |  |
|  |  |
|  |  |
|  |  |
|  |  |
|  |  |

Now let's describe God and Jesus:

| Describe God using 10 adjectives | Describe Jesus using 10 adjectives |
|---|---|
|  |  |
|  |  |
|  |  |
|  |  |
|  |  |
|  |  |
|  |  |
|  |  |
|  |  |
|  |  |

**Compare your word lists for Father/Mother and God/Jesus. Do you see any similarities? Any differences?**




**Are your descriptions of God and Jesus the same? How are they different? What do you notice about your word choices?**




**Do you feel more comfortable with Jesus or Father God? Explain.**




Read John 14:8-10. Write out verse 9b:

**Write out Hebrews 1:3a:**


**According to these verses, is there any difference in character between God and Jesus?**


If our view of God doesn't line up with the truth of Scripture, then we have a perception problem. God does not change. *Jesus Christ is the same yesterday and today and forever* (Hebrews 13:8).

Throughout Scripture, God revealed Himself in many different ways and by many different names. In this important way, He revealed wonderful aspects of His character.

If you've been a Christ Follower for any length of time, you will likely be very familiar with God's character. Please don't rush through this. We can know God's character in a textbook way and yet completely miss what it means for us personally. We can't truly know who *we* are without knowing who **He is**!

**Write out the following Scriptures:**

*God is...Approachable*

**Vine's Expository Dictionary**
**Approach**: *to draw near, literally and physically; figuratively of drawing near to God*

**Ephesians 3:11-12**


**Hebrews 4:15-16**


**James 4:8**


**How is it possible to approach God? Who made the way possible for us?**

**In what manner can you approach God with your sexual past? Your brokenness?**


**Is there any requirement for approaching God?**


*God is...Forgiving*

**Easton's Bible Dictionary**
**Forgiveness of God:** *In pardoning sin, God absolves the sinner from the condemnation of the law, and that on account of the work of Christ, i.e., he removes the guilt of sin, or the sinner's actual liability to eternal wrath on account of it. All sins are forgiven freely. The sinner is by this act of grace forever freed from the guilt and penalty of his sins. This is the peculiar prerogative of God. It is offered to all in the gospel.*

**Psalm 103:12**


**Matthew 26:28**


**Acts 13:38-39**


**Colossians 1:13-14**


**Through what and whom have our sins been forgiven? (Matthew 26:28)**


**Are we required to do anything to receive God's forgiveness? (Acts 13:38—39)**

### *God...makes us Clean*

**Vine's Expository Dictionary**
**Purify:** *to cleanse from defilement; morally, the heart, the soul*

**Psalm 51:1-4**

**1 John 1:9**

**Hebrews 9:14**

If sin makes our heart unclean/defiled, what is our remedy? (Hebrews 9:14)

Sometimes we argue that our choices aren't hurting anyone. Is that true? (Psalm 51)

What is God's promise to those who confess their sins? (1 John 1:9)

### *God is...Just*

**Easton's Bible Dictionary**
**Justice:** *Rendering to everyone that which is his due. It has been distinguished from equity in this respect that while justice means merely doing what positive law demands, equity means the doing of what is fair and right in every separate case.*

**Psalm 89:14**

Psalm 103:6


Isaiah 30:18


The word "oppressed" means to *crush or burden by abuse of power or authority*. List ways you have been oppressed by your sexual past.


What is God's promise to those who are oppressed?


If you've been a victim of abuse/sexual assault, does God promise a timeline for justice?


💡 My "I Get it!" thought for today:

## Reflections: Yours, Mine & the Truth

### *Day 4: He's the Fairest One of All*

Are you in awe of your Maker yet? No one can compare to Him. He's flawless in every way. More majestic than a rare diamond is Jesus our Savior. My hope during this entire journey is connecting our head to our heart. We can know truth in our heads, but sometimes it gets stuck there without filtering down to our hearts.

Our past *has* affected our beliefs about God, which causes truth to get lodged in our head rather than our heart. Pain, tragedy, and a whole lot of things beyond our understanding can impact our view of God until it becomes distorted, like that funhouse mirror we talked about in our homework on Day 2.

Sister, isn't it time to shed the Light on that funhouse mirror image of God and see Him as He truly is? There's *so* much more to learn.

**Let's pray:** *Lord, I want to see You as You are. Not a warped image of You. Not Truth in parts or pieces of my choosing. Where I'm in the dark, please turn on the Light! In Jesus' Name. Amen.*

Write out the following Scriptures as we explore more of God's amazing attributes.

### *God is...Love*

**Torrey's Topical Text**
**Love:** *Part of God's character. Described as sovereign, great, abiding, unfailing, unalienable, constraining, and everlasting; irrespective of merit. It is exhibited in the giving of Christ, His death on the cross, adoption, redemption, forgiveness, drawing us to Himself, discipline, and the defeating of evil counsels.*

**Vine's Expository Dictionary**
*Love can be known only from the actions it prompts. God's love is seen in the gift of His Son.*

### John 3:16

### 1 John 3:1

### Hosea 11:4

### Romans 5:6-8

**Romans 8:38-39**

**In what ways has God revealed His love to mankind?**

**What word picture does God reveal in Hosea 11:4 to describe His tender love? In what ways have you felt God's tender love?**

**In what ways did you "perform" for others in order to receive their love?**

**In what ways have you been performing to earn God's love?**

**Is there anything in your past that separated you from God's love?**

*God is...Good*

**Easton's Bible Dictionary**
**Goodness (of God):** *A perfection of His character which He exercises towards His creatures according to their various circumstances and relations. In respect to the miseries of His creatures, it is mercy, compassion; in the case of impenitent sinners, long-suffering patience; on favor upon the unworthy, it is grace. God is infinitely and unchangeably good, and His goodness is incomprehensible by the finite mind. God's goodness appears in two things: giving and forgiving.*

**Psalm 25:8**

**Psalm 86:5**

**Jeremiah 32:41**

**John 10:11, 14**

**List 5—10 ways God has shown His goodness to you:**

**Write the painful questions you have that may be blocking your belief in God's goodness:** *If He's so good, then why*_____?

If you've been the victim of sexual assault, how did God preserve you despite your past? (Think of special relationships, hobbies, activities, etc.)

*God is...Faithful*

**Easton's Bible Dictionary**
**Faithful:** *Steadfast, dedicated, dependable, and worthy of trust. It is used of God's word or covenant as true and to be trusted.*

**Psalm 33:4**

**Lamentations 3:22-23**

1 Corinthians 10:13

1 Thessalonians 5:23-25

**In what ways has God shown you compassion in regard to your sexual past?**

**What concerns do you have about living your present/future free from sexual sin? What is God's promise to you? (1 Cor. 10:13, 1 Thess. 5:23-25)**

    Woven together, these truths tell us a story—a true story—that we can believe. God IS who He says He is. And He will DO what He says He will do! God is faithful to His own Word, and He uses His very nature *for* us and not against us.

Pray aloud this declaration:
    God's word is right and true. (Ps. 33:4) Because God is true to His laws, He will afflict me in faithfulness and love (Ps. 119:75) as any good parent would do for an unruly child. In spite of my painful affliction for the waywardness of my choices, I can count on His great love and compassion (Lam. 3:22-23) because His deep well of faithfulness will never run dry. Moreover, God helps me from sinning more. He helps me to overcome temptations and even gives me open doors of escape. (1 Cor. 10:13) In fact, God is so committed to my sanctification that He is able to keep my whole spirit, soul, and body blameless when Christ appears. God's clarion call is to set me free from the bondage of my sexual past. Best of all, **He will do it!** (1 Thess. 5:23—25)

 **My "I Get It!" thought for today is:**

## Reflections: Yours, Mine & the Truth

### Day 5: Living Beyond the Label

Merchandising labels have power. You might not have noticed how much influence labels have on your buying. But savvy marketers know exactly the power and influence they have over your spending.

Food labels tell us about a product and reveal the good, the bad, and the ugly. Is it good for me and my family? Will it contribute to good health or not? Some labels give warnings of potential danger if ingested or harmful long-term effects.

Clothing labels tell us what the garment is made of and how to care for it. For many fashionistas, it's ALL about *The Label*—the designer label. Good money is paid for The Label too. In fact, The Label can make us look like we have it all together whether we do or not.

There's another label we can put on too. It happened when we least expected it. Just one glance in that soul-mirror and the Enemy used hurtful words and the pain of our past to label us. These soul-labels become like heavy chains around our hearts, keeping us in darkness.

If we don't know how God sees us, then we're liable to accept those cruel and hurtful labels.
> Adulteress
> > Stupid
> > > Worthless
> > > > Shameful
> > > > > Unloveable
> > > > > > Unwanted
> > > > > > > Broken beyond repair

**What soul-labels have you been hiding under?**




Are you ready for a reality check? As you dig into the truth of how God sees you, you'll be on your way to one amazing makeover. But before we get started on today's lesson, let's ask God, the Ultimate Designer, to reconstruct our view of ourselves according to His marvelous intention.

> **Let's pray:** *God, You are the Fountain of Life, the Light by which I see (Psalm 36:8) and the Designer of my being (Psalm 139:13-16). Help me to see myself with Your eyes of grace and to receive Your love today. In Jesus' Name. Amen.*

**Think about your Heavenly Father. How does He label you?**




It might surprise you to know how He *really* sees you. Read the verses in the following chart and underline the parts that reveal how God sees YOU. This list is not all-inclusive; you are this and so much more!

| The **Real** Me...in Christ | |
|---|---|
| Yet to all who did receive Him, to those who believed in His name, He gave the right to become children of God. | John 1:12 |
| Now if we are children, then we are heirs—heirs of God and co-heirs with Christ, if indeed we share in His sufferings in order that we may also share in His glory. | Romans 8:17 |
| I no longer call you servants, because a servant does not know his master's business. Instead, I have called you friends, for everything that I learned from my Father I have made known to you. | John 15:15 |
| You were bought at a price... | 1 Cor. 6:20a |
| Therefore there is now no condemnation for those who are in Christ Jesus, because through Christ Jesus the law of the Spirit who gives life has set you free from the law of sin and of death. | Roman 8:1-2 |
| For he has rescued us from the dominion of darkness and brought us into the kingdom of the Son he loves, in whom we have redemption, the forgiveness of sins. | Colossians 1:13-14 |
| He predestined us for adoption to sonship through Jesus Christ, in accordance with His pleasure and will. | Ephesians 1:5 |
| Therefore, if anyone is in Christ, the new creation has come: The old has gone, the new is here! | 2 Cor. 5:17 |
| And He has committed to us the message of reconciliation. We are therefore Christ's ambassadors... | 2 Cor. 5:19b-20 |
| ...and in Christ you have been brought to fullness. He is the head over every power and authority. | Col. 2:10 |
| For you died, and your life is now hidden with Christ in God. | Col. 3:3 |
| For we are God's handiwork, created in Christ Jesus to do good works, which God prepared in advance for us to do. | Eph. 2:10 |
| No, in all these things we are more than conquerors through him who loved us. | Romans 8:37 |

| For You created my inmost being; You knit me together in my mother's womb. I praise You, for I am fearfully and wonderfully made; wonderful are Your works. I know that full well. | Ps 139:13-14 |
|---|---|
| "You are the salt of the earth...You are the light of the world." | Matt. 5:13a, 14a |
| What, then, shall we say in response to these things? If God is for us, who can be against us? | Rom. 8:31 |
| Now it is God who makes both us and you stand firm in Christ. He anointed us, set his seal of ownership on us, and put his Spirit in our hearts as a deposit, guaranteeing what is to come. | 2 Cor. 1:21-22 |
| I can do all this through Him who gives me strength. | Phil 4:13 |
| Therefore, since we have been justified by faith, we have peace with God through our Lord Jesus Christ. | Romans 5:1 |

**Let's go back to a question I asked you earlier in this segment and answer it again. How does God label you? Did your answer change?**

**Look up one final verse. Write out Isaiah 1:18.**

No matter what you've done or what you've endured, that cloak of shame is not yours to wear. Go ahead and take a good look at yourself in the mirror.
*You're beautiful.*

 **My "I Get It!" thought for today:**

# Chapter 3: Hearing from God

# Hearing from God

---

*Day 1: Can You Hear Me Now?*

"*Can you hear me now?*"

Many of us may remember this popular slogan by a well-known cell phone company that boasted the ability of its users to get reception even in the remotest locations.

Perhaps that's been your mantra as you've cried out to God with your questions, pain, and grief. Rest assured, my friend, He *sees* you and He *hears* you. Your enemy, the devil, prowls around like a lion, seeking whom he may devour (1 Peter 5:8). Scripture also says the devil is a thief who comes to steal, kill, and destroy (John 10:10). Believe me when I tell you that the devil wants **nothing** good for you. He wants to devour your faith. He wants to steal your quiet/alone time with God and keep you trapped in busyness. He wants to kill any hope that God cares about you. And he wants to destroy your life by keeping you in bondage to your shame and grief.

**But that's about to change.**

That's if you're *ready* for the change—the makeover—that we talked about in the last chapter. Change will require you to surrender old ways of thinking. It will require you to identify the lies you've believed and exchange them for the Truth of God's Word.

> **Let's pray:** *God, I'm tired of feeling devoured and destroyed. I won't allow myself to be ripped off or ripped up anymore. Help me to stand up and stand strong. I will believe who You say that You are. Help me in my unbelief. Give me ears to hear You so that my life reveals You through and through. In Jesus' Name. Amen.*

Most of us are familiar with the passage of Scripture about Sarah trying to manipulate the timing of God's promised child to her and Abraham. But there's another character in this story that I want to bring under the magnifying glass. Her name is Hagar. She's Sarah's servant and Abraham's mistress in a not-so-perfect-plan. And despite the relational upheaval that followed, Hagar is under the magnifying glass of God's watchful eye.

**Read Genesis 16:1-13. Look back again at verses 8, 11, 13 and sum them up in your own words.**

Can you imagine how Hagar felt after that brief conversation with God? It was going to take everything she had to go back and face a situation from which she had run. How would you feel after an intimate encounter like that with God? She knew God heard her. And she knew God saw her. Her faith was soaring. It had restored her hope and settled within her a peace that passed all understanding. In spite of her circumstances, ill-treatment and hopelessness, God met her where she was.

**What circumstances (past or present) do you need assurance from God that He has seen and heard? (As a child? Adolescent? Adult?)**

**Read Genesis 21:1-20, paying special attention to verse 17.**

When we last saw Hagar, we learned that she tended to run away when faced with problems. Now, she's been sent away—rejected. God declared that the promised child would come through Sarah—and he (Isaac) was born to Sarah in her old age. In spite of the turn of events in the relational triangle between Abraham, Sarah, and Hagar, God hadn't forgotten about Hagar. She never left His gaze. He cared for her and Ishmael. God still had a plan.
**Write out Genesis 21:17:**

**Write out the following Scriptures and look for common words:**

**Psalm 10:17**

**Psalm 17:1**

**Psalm 18:6**

**Psalm 34:17**

**Psalm 55:17**

Maybe like Hagar you've been rejected. Rejected by parents, husband, boyfriend, boss, or friend. No matter how desperate or crushing your experiences have made you feel, let God's truth resound:

**"Do not be afraid! I have heard you crying…"**

 **My "I Get It!" thought for today:**

## Hearing from God

*Day 2: Talk to Me*

Before I married, I had a solid time with God every morning. I set my alarm at 5:00 a.m. and sat with Him for at least one hour, if not longer. It was sweet time with God. I'd wait quietly before Him and allow Him to guide my Scripture reading. Other times, I followed a reading plan from a devotional book. Sometimes I journaled my prayers, and other times I'd speak them out. I'd journal what I felt He was teaching me, as well as significant events in my life. Sometimes I listened quietly to worship music, and other times I'd sing to Him. One thing is sure. I coveted that time with God. During our intimate time together, my faith grew deeper and deeper. I was in *love*!

After I married, my schedule was totally thrown off. Now I had this man walking about the house making noise, making coffee, and totally interrupting my quiet! And if that wasn't challenging enough, our first child entered the scene 14 months later. Her brother came 19 months after that. Pretty soon, my quiet world was anything but quiet, and I felt desperate to find my normal again. I was thrilled to be married, and I loved our babies the moment I discovered I was pregnant. But midnight feedings and interrupted sleep did a number on my time with God. I felt like I was drifting out to sea, and I needed my Anchor to ground me again. I couldn't function without Him, much less minister to anyone else.

After time, I remember noticing that despite being enormously fatigued, I kept waking up at the same time each morning. I had the comforting sense that God was telling me that He missed our time together as much as I did. I'd try to drag myself out of bed but instead chose to hit the snooze again. After several weeks, I cried out to Him in desperation, *"God, I'm so sorry. I did it again! Please don't give up on me."*

Shortly after 2:00 a.m. the next morning, I heard the doorbell ring. It woke me out of a **dead** sleep. I figured a neighbor was in trouble and needed help. (I'm not sure why I didn't wake my husband to check things out.) I went to the door, and no one was there. The outdoor motion detector wasn't lit, which indicated no one had come onto the property. But I knew what I heard! Sister, if I didn't hear something, I would have still been sleeping!

I went back to bed, and my mind went into overdrive. I began to feel afraid. I lay there while my husband was sound asleep. I prayed for protection over my family, prayed for others, counted herds of sheep, and played my A—Z names of God game in my head. After a long while, I fell asleep again. Then came my 5:00 a.m. alarm. I hit snooze and thought, *"God, I know what we talked about yesterday, but You can't possibly expect me to get up after what happened in the wee hours this morning!"* Within a few minutes, my resolve kicked in, and I rolled out of bed.

With Bible in hand, I sat down at the kitchen table and bowed my head. I prayed, *"God, I don't even know where to start. Please help me."* As He'd done so many times before, a Scripture address came to my mind. I had no idea what it said. It was Matthew 14:27.

> **But Jesus immediately said to them:**
> **"Take courage! It is I. Don't be afraid."**

You can call me crazy, but I know in my know-er that Jesus rang my doorbell. After getting freaked out in the night, I believed this was His assurance that it was really Him. *He* had come to me. My sweet Savior had come to me *again*. I sat there with my head bowed, tears of joy and gratitude spilling onto the table. Joy, because it was Him all along; gratitude, because I could have missed this blessing had I stayed in bed. I whispered, *"Lord, thank You! Thank You for coming. I love You so much."*

**Read Matthew 14:28-29 and write who said what in the following space:**

**Peter:**


**Jesus:**


Regardless of what you've done in the past, or what has been done to you, God wants to come to you and talk with you. You need not fear Him. He is "gentle and humble in heart, and you will find rest for your souls" (Matthew 11:29).

His words are life (John 6:68). He is not a Band-Aid. He is the Healer. Remember this: there is no real, lasting healing apart from God. It starts with a relationship with Him. Maybe you've been searching for "something." Maybe you've been trying out different religions for something that makes sense. Maybe you're desperately hanging on, and you need to be rescued. Or maybe you've been away from God, and you're up to your knees in mud, and you want to come back to Him. There's no time like the present. If that's you, I invite you to pray the following:

*Dear Jesus, I believe You are the Son of God, and that makes You GOD. I believe You died for me and paid a debt I couldn't pay myself. I believe You resurrected from the dead and ascended into Heaven. I accept Your forgiveness for all my sins – past, present, and future. Thank You for the free gift of salvation and a life in Heaven with God. Help me to live all my days for You. In Jesus' Name. Amen.*

The following verse makes me weep with gratitude and love for my God every time I read it:
*Hear me as I pray, O LORD. Be merciful and answer me!*
*My heart has heard You say, "Come and talk with Me."*
*And my heart responds, "LORD, I am coming."*
Psalm 27:7-8 NLT

Use the space below to write out *your* heart response to God:

 **My "I Get It!" thought for today:**

# Hearing from God

## Day 3: Defining your Time with God

Strengthening your relationship with God will make all the difference in your daily living, and especially as you seek healing and peace for your sexual past. Whether you prefer to call it Quiet Time, Personal Time, or Devotional Time—be sure to make it non-negotiable time! Settle it in your mind that you won't exchange it for anything else. Elevate it above all else in your day. In today's lesson, we'll talk about how to make that a reality.

For some, spending time with God is already a routine part of your day. For others, this may be something you have wanted to do or know you should be doing but haven't had success. And yet for others, it may be a new idea that you hadn't considered before. Don't be discouraged if you find yourself in the latter two camps. You can change that *today*.

> **Let's pray:** *God, I want to know You better. Help me to want what You want and to obey as You lead me. Give me the desire and the power to do what pleases You. Help me want to do Your will. (Phil 2:13) In Jesus' Name. Amen.*

**Here are five simple steps to having a personal time with God:**

1. **Find a special place where you will meet with God daily.** If possible, this should be an area that is separate from your regular living space. It's reserved just for your time with God. Your special place can also be outdoors. God often speaks to me through creation and nature walks. Scripture records Jesus spending time with God on a mountainside, in an olive grove, a garden, and in solitary/lonely places. For me, my special place is a recliner in our family room. I keep an iPod on a small table next to the chair where I also keep my Bible, journal, a few devotional books, pens, and highlighters. This is an area that I keep separate from other activities I enjoy doing (like reading, watching TV, etc.).

2. **Firm up a time to meet with God.** Ideally, this is a routine time each day. Whether morning, afternoon, or evening, it should be a time of day in which you feel fresh. For me, early mornings are best because the house is quiet, my head is clear, and I can focus on God before I get involved in my day.

3. **Fill your mouth with praise.** Begin your time with God by thanking Him for who He is. In the previous chapter, you discovered some amazing things about God. Start there, and thank Him for being the embodiment of those glorious attributes. Or consider singing to Him. *He put a new song in my mouth, a hymn of praise to our God* (Psalm 40:3a). You're singing to an audience of One, and He thinks you sound pretty terrific, so don't worry whether you can carry a tune or not.

4. **Focus and apply God's Word to your life.** *"Accept, LORD, the willing praise of my mouth, and teach me Your laws."* (Psalm 119:108) Your praise prepares your heart to receive from God as we see in the Scripture above. Read a Scripture or a short passage of Scripture and journal what God is speaking to you. For me, I notice that I sometimes "bump" into a word or phrase that piques my interest. As I read it over and over (meditate on it), I will sense God speaking to me through it. I might even spend a couple of days reading the same passage until I "get it." Reading an entire book of the Bible in one sitting doesn't mean you've had a great personal time with God. We eat one bite at a time. Quality trumps quantity.

5. **Follow His ways.** *"My sheep listen to My voice; I know them, and they follow Me"* (John 10:27). After you have focused on God's Word—digesting what you sense He is feeding you—ask yourself how you can apply that truth to your life. Then do it! That's where the "following" part comes into play.

   As we journey deeper and deeper into this study, God will be showing you many things. Some of those things will require the action of hearing God and then following His ways.

You may be wondering, *"But how do I know if I'm really **hearing** God?"* We're coming to that part, but for now, use the Checklist below to get you in a position to hear from the One True God.

## MEETING WITH GOD CHECKLIST

☐ **Find a place to meet with God daily.**
My place will be _____
Notes: _____
_____

☐ **Firm up a time to meet with God.**
My time to meet with God will be _____
Notes: _____
_____

☐ **Fill my mouth with praise.**
I have warmed up my vocal cords for a worshipful concert!
Notes: _____
_____

☐ **Focus and apply God's Word to my life.**
I have a journal to write down what I believe God is saying to me. I have a reading plan to follow if I need it.
Notes: _____
_____
_____

☐ **Follow His ways.**
I will follow God's ways with His help! Today's date: _____
Notes: _____
_____

 **My "I Get It!" thought for today:**

# Hearing from God

## *Day 4: Heart Prep*

Yesterday we discussed what spending time with God daily may look like. Hopefully, your checklists are completed, and you're ready to get started. God is more ready to meet with you than you can imagine. Let us consider a few "heart conditions" for hearing from God. Scripture tells us:

*If I had cherished sin in my heart, the Lord would not have listened.*
Psalm 66:18

The word *cherish* means *"to nurture; to keep or cultivate with care and affection. To entertain or harbor in the mind deeply and resolutely."*

We won't hear clearly from God if we refuse to give up bitterness, unforgiveness, and the like. These things aren't easy to lay down, but God will honor your steps forward, however small they may be.

> **Let's pray:** *Father, thank You for Your grace and mercy. Thank You for receiving me with joy and goodness. I want my heart to be in good condition before You. I trust in Your faithfulness and love to mend my heart. Give me courage to be honest with You. In Jesus' Name. Amen.*

That we **can** come near to God is His gift of mercy toward the afflicted.

*Therefore, since we have a Great High Priest who has ascended into heaven, Jesus the Son of God, let us hold firmly to the faith we profess. For we do not have a High Priest who is unable to empathize with our weaknesses, but we have One who has been tempted in every way, just as we are – yet He did not sin. Let us then approach God's throne of grace with confidence, so that we may receive mercy and find grace to help us in our time of need* (Hebrews 4:14-16 NIV).

What does this mean for us? It means that Jesus, our High Priest, has opened the way for us to the Father. Because of Christ, we can approach God's throne boldly—without disguise, camouflage, mask, or cover-up. His throne is a throne of grace, and it brings Him *joy* in our coming.

We can come *freely*. Isn't that amazing? More amazing is that He *receives* us gladly. If we want to hear Him speak to us and find direction and healing in our life, we need to have a right heart before Him.

We will examine five key areas to preparing our hearts to hear from God:

 **Humility & Surrender**

In her book **FOREVER RUINED FOR THE ORDINARY**, Joy Dawson says, *"Pride feels no need to inquire of God and take time to seek His face. It is both proud and foolish to live independently of Him by continuously making our own decisions and hoping or presuming they are His will."*[1]

Look up the following verses and note what you learn about humility.

**Psalm 25:9**

**Proverbs 22:4**

**1 Peter 5:5**

**Philippians 2:5-9**

**Think of a time you humbled yourself before God or someone else. How did your humility change the situation?**

**Think of a time your pride got you in trouble. What happened?**

### 🗝 Honesty & Truthfulness

To find healing from our sexual past, it is going to take honesty and truthfulness. We cannot make excuses, deny the truth, stuff the truth, or lie to ourselves any longer. Nor can we lie to God about it. He already knows the truth.

**John 8:32**

**Psalm 145:18**

**Jeremiah 5:3**

**Psalm 51:6**




**Has there been a time in your life when God was showing you something about yourself and you refused to acknowledge or deal with it? What was the outcome?**

 Faith & Belief

We have to believe that God **is** the answer for our sin, our forgiveness, and our healing. The basis for our faith is the character of God. He *is* who He says He is. Faith believes that He will *do* what He says He will do. If you stumble in this area, meditate on His awesome attributes from Chapter 2.

**Look up the following verses and write what you learn about faith.**

**Hebrews 11:6**



**Matthew 21:22**



**Luke 1:45**



**Romans 4:18**



**Psalm 101:6**

**Reread that last Scripture again. Had you ever considered that exercising your faith would actually** *minister* **to God? What does that mean to you?**

**Think of a time when you took a step of faith with God into an unknown situation. What happened?**

 A Yielded Will

A yielded will is a surrendered will. It's a mind that makes way or grants preference to. This is often difficult because we want our own way.

Here's an example we can all relate to: If I'm driving my car and come to a yield sign, I must yield. I don't think twice about it. That sign is not posted there as a suggestion, but a command. What if I didn't yield? What if I decided to take my chances, bullying my way through traffic to get ahead first? Chances are pretty likely that I could get in a serious collision. An unyielded heart collides with His.

**Look up the following Scriptures and notice the difference between God's way and man's way:**

**Proverbs 14:12**

**Psalm 18:30**

**Psalm 25:8**

**Do you find it easy or difficult to yield or "give way" to another? To God? Think of an example and write the result of that situation here:**

**Obedience**

Obedience and a yielded will are sisters. A yielded will involves the mind; obedience involves the heart. We can acknowledge with a nod of the head that God's paths are right and true, but it's another thing altogether to put it into action. That's where obedience comes in. Obedience to God's ways always involves action—*doing* what He says.

**In the following verses, note the outcome of obedience or disobedience:**

Matthew 21:28-31

Jeremiah 7:23

Romans 6:16

John 14:23

**What did you learn about obedience from the above verses?**

**Let's honestly assess ourselves. Which area(s) are most difficult for you?**

- ☐ Come to God in humility
- ☐ Come to God in honesty
- ☐ Come to God in faith
- ☐ Come to God with a yielded will
- ☐ Come to God in obedience

So how did you do on your checkup? Do you need our Great Physician to do a little surgery? Don't despair. He is gentle and kind and never rushes the process. He is committed to you and will finish the work that He began in you (Phil. 1:6).

**Pray and ask God to help you in those area(s) now. Write out your confession:**

 My "I Get It!" thought for today:

## Hearing from God

### *Day 5: The Ways that God Speaks*

Two days ago, we ended our homework with the question: *"How do I know I'm really hearing from God?"*

From the time I was a child, I have experienced a handful of God-encounters that were so amazing they have been forever etched into my memory. Even still, after I came to know Christ in a personal way, I've sometimes felt as though God and I were communicating on two different radio frequencies. And quite frankly, we do! Scripture says, *"For My thoughts are not your thoughts, neither are your ways My ways,"* declares the LORD (Isaiah 55:8 NIV). Someone is going to have to change her radio frequency so that communication is clear. That someone is me, and mostly it's also you.

In 1999, I sensed God drawing me into missions. My first outreach was to India in 2000. Through my church, I became connected to Mission Bridge, a ministry under Youth With A Mission (YWAM). The purpose of Mission Bridge was to prepare short-term teams for the mission field. I learned that preparation is not merely limited to lining up ministry opportunities with indigenous workers, but it was more about preparing our *hearts* by examining our motives, uncovering areas of pride, and submitting to leadership. It was also about intercession, hearing the voice of God, and exchanging our agendas for God's. Our preparation for that trip to India was anything but dull. It began the most thrilling adventure of learning to hear and follow God's voice! What God did on that outreach is for another book, but it forever changed my view of God.

Several Christian women have admitted to me that they are unsure about hearing God's direction on any given matter. Hear me, friend: God is *always* speaking, and He wants to show you the way to peace, healing, joy, and more. He assures us that *"My sheep listen to My voice; I know them, and they follow Me"* (John 10:27).

**Let's pray:** *God, I want to know You. Your words are life and truth. Teach me Your ways. Fine tune my hearing. Give me understanding to see that You've been speaking to me all along. In Jesus' Name. Amen.*

**Write out 2 Timothy 3:16**




The book **FOREVER RUINED FOR THE ORDINARY** by Joy Dawson deeply impacted my relationship with God and helped me to hear His directives in my life more clearly. In her book, Joy lists many ways God speaks:

### God Speaks Through His Word[2]
1. When we read it (Psalm 119:24)
2. When it is in literature
3. When being quoted through ministries of preaching and teaching, shared testimonies, or music
4. When specific portions are given by a person of proven character and ministry who has been directed by the Holy Spirit to do so to an individual or group
5. When we receive revelation by the Holy Spirit through meditation on the Word
6. When communicated on billboards, TV, or radio
7. When it has been memorized and then quickened by the Holy Spirit to meet a need
8. When the Holy Spirit speaks a Scripture reference (book, chapter, and at times, the verse) to our minds which specifically addresses a given situation

**God Speaks Through What We See**[3]
1. Visions (Acts 10:3)
2. Dreams (Genesis 37; Genesis 41; Daniel 2:1; Matthew 2:20)
3. Angels (nearly 100 references in Scripture about angelic visits)
4. Writing with His finger (Exodus 31:18; Daniel 5:24; John 8:6-9)
5. Rainbows (Genesis 8:21-22)
6. Creation (Psalm 19:1-4; Romans 1:20)
7. Pillar of Fire and Pillar of Cloud (Exodus 13:21)
8. A Consuming Fire (Exodus 24:17)
9. Supernatural Signs (Isaiah 38; 1 Samuel 14:10; Judges 6-7)
10. Circumstances
    **NOTE**: *Many people take circumstances as one of the most obvious and reliable means of interpreting God's will, but it should be one of the ways we should least expect Him to guide us. Circumstances can be the result of our poor choices; they can be engineered by satanic forces to keep us from God's highest purposes in our lives; they can be a means of God's testing us; or they can simply be the result of other people's presumptions, no matter how sincere they may be. We must not presume that a string of favorable circumstances is necessarily a sign from God that we are on the right track in relation to His will and purposes, although they can be.*
11. Casting lots (Joshua 8:8-10; Acts 1:23-26)
12. Urim and Thumin (Exodus 28:30; Numbers 27:21)

**God Speaks Through Our Hearing**[4]
1. Directly into our thoughts (John 10:27, 34; Genesis 16:13; Exodus 20:1; Jeremiah 30:2; John 9:29; Acts 10:15; Hebrews 4:7)
2. Audible voice (Acts 9:4-6)
3. A word of prophecy (2 Kings 5:26-27; Acts 5)
4. Music and poetry (Psalms)
5. Other people (1 Samuel 25:23-31; 2 Samuel 12:1-12; 1 Kings 13)
6. The Animal Kingdom (Numbers 22:28-30)
7. Testimonies (John 1:40-42; John 4:5-42; Luke 8:26-39)

**God Speaks Through Impressions to Our Spirits**[5]
1. A strong conviction of peace (Romans 8:6; Colossians 3:15)
2. Constraints and Restraints of the Holy Spirit (Acts 16:6-7)

Are you surprised by all the ways He speaks? I hope you took on the challenge and looked up some or all of the Scriptures noted above. As you come to know His character and ways better, you will grow in confidence in recognizing His voice. As you know Him, you will trust Him. He spoke to His people long ago, and He still speaks to us today. And we can trust that He will speak with us tomorrow. *Jesus Christ is the same yesterday and today and forever* (Hebrews 13:8).

**What did you learn about the ways in which God speaks? Did anything surprise you?**

**In what ways are you recognizing His voice in your life?**

Journaling is an excellent means of recording what you believe God is saying to you. Some people journal every day, others do not. Personally, I don't journal every day and only record significant things I believe He is saying to me. I've recorded numerous instructions through His Word, dreams, divine appointments, special events, and more. I'm constantly amazed that His Spirit lives in me and talks to me!

Hearing and following is an adventure greater and more fulfilling than any extreme sport in which you could participate! My spiritual mentor, Mary Kay Wagner, has said on many occasions: *"Notice what you notice!"*

Begin a deeper adventure with Him today. Notice what you notice. Chances are He's speaking to you.

 **My "I GET IT!" thought for today:**

# Chapter 4:
# Search & Rescue

# Search & Rescue

*Day 1: The Search for Significance*

On that long flight to Russia when I was brought face to Face with my sin, I was well aware that God had not only peeked into my emotional baggage, but had opened it wide for a better view.

I quickly shut the book. There was nowhere to run. Nowhere to hide. And no parachute with which to jump out of the plane.

Stuffed in my baggage were…

Lies  
Denial  
Blame  
Shame  
Mistrust  
Self-hatred  
Sexual promiscuity  
*And my larger-than-life "Secret"*

Although frightened about the depth of pain and dysfunction that lay stuffed in my bag, I knew it had to be unpacked, not only for my emotional and spiritual well-being, but for the success of my present relationships and those yet to come. I knew that no matter how painful the process, I could trust myself to God. So with great fear of the unknown, my healing process began in the arctic cold of Russia.

Mary DeMuth, author of **Live Uncaged** says, *"Healing erupts in the light of truth. Simply put, if we hide things, we fester. But if we want Jesus to uncage us, we have to tell the truth."*[1]

**What about you? What's stuffed in your bag? Is it abuse? Control? Eating disorders? Emotional or extra-marital affairs? Drugs or alcohol? Pornography? Promiscuous sex? Abortion? Shame?**

You may feel overwhelmed at all you have buried deep in your baggage, but God is not. He is able to set you free and bring peace and joy to your life.

**Let's pray:** *God, today is the day I'm claiming my baggage–the bad, the ugly, and the ugliest. I'm going to stop denying and lying that my past isn't affecting me. Use my past as a stage to display Your remarkable power. In Jesus' Name. Amen.*

Part of exposing our "baggage" is coming to grips with the truth that we've searched for love, acceptance—some*one* or some*thing*—to fill a need within our soul. Except our search went terribly wrong. The only thing we *found* was momentary pleasure that faded into heartache, pain, mistrust, and deeper emptiness.

**Write out the following verses and underline any part in which you can personally identify.**

**Lamentations 1:2**

**Hosea 2:7a**

**Song of Solomon 3:1-2**

John and Stasi Eldredge, authors of **Captivating: Unveiling the Mystery of a Woman's Soul**, suggest that deep within her heart, a woman was made for romance, made to play an irreplaceable role in a shared adventure, and possesses a beauty all her own to unveil...because she bears the image of God.[2] (And by the way, our beauty has nothing to do with makeup, Botox, or the scale.)

Our search for love and acceptance often leads us into severe image issues. It can also lead us into the arms of lovers who we hope will love us better than the last one did. After a relationship ends we may admit that we were looking for love in all the wrong places. But if we're honest with ourselves, I think we really mean that we looked for love in the wrong *arms*. Our soul craves intimacy, but we don't know where or how to satisfy its hunger. We reduce intimacy to the bedroom and love to a feeling. And when the fire of those flames dies down, The Search goes on.

Could it be that we've been trying to fill our need for intimacy in the wrong ways? Searching for significance in the wrong places?

Searching in the wrong places will always—*without fail*—leave an ache in the heart. Our desperate need for purpose, love, and acceptance leads us to take matters into our own hands. The results, of course, are disastrous. With every hookup or breakup, our hearts get hardened. After all, we have to protect ourselves, right? Let's go look back to the beginning and find out where we took a wrong turn.

**Read Genesis 3:1-13 in the New Living Translation (NLT). Write out the first sentence in verse 6.**

Authors John and Stasi Eldredge offer, "The woman was *convinced*. That's it? Just like that? In a matter of moments? Convinced of what? Look in your own heart and you'll see. Convinced that God was holding out on her. Convinced that she could not trust His heart toward her. Convinced that in order to have the best possible life, she must take matters into her own hands. And so she did."[3]

**Read Genesis 3:16-18**


**In your own words, what was the curse God pronounced on Adam and Eve?**


John and Stasi Eldredge share the following insights:

> "The curse on Adam cannot be limited *only* to thorns and thistles. If that were so, men with white-collar jobs would escape the curse. No, *every* son of Adam would now be cursed with *futility* and *failure*. Life will be hard in the place he'll feel it most. Failure is a man's worst fear.

> "In the same way, the curse for Eve and all her daughters cannot be limited *only* to babies and marriage. If that were so, every single woman without children would escape the curse. The meaning is deeper and the implications are for *every* daughter of Eve. Woman is cursed with loneliness (relational heartache), with the urge to control (especially her man), and with the dominance of men (which is not how things were supposed to be). And every woman knows now that she is not what she was meant to be. And she fears that soon it will be known—if it hasn't *already* been discovered—and that she will be abandoned. That is a woman's worst fear—*abandonment*."[4]

Can you relate?

The Search for Significance can cause us to stray far, far away until the All-Sufficient One rescues us from a distant place. Only then can we sing, *"...I found the one my heart loves..."* (Song of Solomon 3:4).

Let me remind you of what Mary DeMuth said: *"Healing erupts in the light of truth."*[5] What light of truth has been revealed to you today? What baggage needs to be exposed?

 **My "I Get It!" thought for today:**

## Search & Rescue

### *Day 2: Searching Among the Rubble*

Yesterday we recognized our Search for Significance—that deep need within the core of our being—for love, acceptance, and purpose. Like Adam and Eve, that search has led us down some dark paths and provided more than a few heartaches. As we pulled back the tree branches and peered into the Garden of Eden, we discovered the essence of the curse upon all the sons and daughters of Adam and Eve.

Today, we'll go on another search, a totally different kind of search. We'll search through our past in order to understand how our views of ourselves, sex, and God have taken shape over the course of our life.

> **Let's pray:** *Father, You are for me and not against me. All my days – past, present, future – are held in Your Mighty hands. Take the futility of my past and cause it to work for my good, as You promise in Romans 8:28. Expose the things hidden in darkness and bring them into Your marvelous Light. In Jesus' Name. Amen.*

Thankfully, I have never experienced the loss of my home to fire, flood, or other disaster, but I know people who have. Our homes hold treasure: photos of our wedding day, the children's growing years, and those of generations past. Jewelry that's tucked away and worn only on special occasions, the treasured memories of Christmas mornings, squeals of laughter, and family gatherings. Every room holds memories, every corridor familiar sounds. Those who have faced such devastating loss mournfully sift the ashes and stumble through the rubble in search of any small token that reminds them of better days and happier times.

As you sift through the ashes of your past and the rubble of your choices, you may not think there is anything worth salvaging among the ash heap. But amidst even the gravest devastation, there is redemption if we look for it. Out of the ashes will emerge beauty—beauty of a soul restored. In your search God will reveal a diamond among the rubble that will change the way you see yourself, your sexuality, and your God.

So what do you say? Shall we let the search begin?

**The next series of questions will help you understand what you learned about sex/sexuality during your growing years.[6] Prayerfully ask God for help.**

**What did you learn about women from your mother?**

**What did you learn about men from your mother?**

**What did you learn about sex from your mother?**

Describe your relationship with your mother as a child, adolescent, and adult.

What did you learn about men from your father?

What did you learn about women from your father?

What did you learn about sex from your father?

Describe your relationship with your father as a child, adolescent, and adult.

Who and/or what influenced your attitudes most about sex? (Describe media, cultural influences, etc.)

As you were growing up, was sex discussed comfortably in your family, or was it a taboo topic? What messages were communicated about sex while you were growing up? Was sex regarded as something special, something worth waiting for? Or was it considered no big deal/a rite of passage?

As a child, how did you feel about being a girl?

**Growing into adulthood, did being female have its advantages or disadvantages? How?**

**What importance did sex have in your relationships? Was it "proof" of love to you or your partner?**

On a separate piece of paper, begin compiling a list of sexual partners: men, women, one-night stands, extramarital affairs, etc. This list will include:
- Emotional and extramarital affairs
- Oral, anal, and vaginal intercourse (including sex with animals)
- Pornographic images in videos, magazines, internet and cell phone
- Phone sex
- Sexual assault and abuse

If you don't know the names of all your partners, make a description of what you do remember, such as: man on vacation with blue t-shirt, etc. Keep this list in a safe place and add to it as God brings people and circumstances to your mind. This is a very important step and one that you cannot go around.

Trudging through the ashes of memories can be a painful experience, but keep pressing in, allowing the Spirit of God to reveal the roots of your attitudes, views, and core beliefs. He *will* reveal. Take His Word for it.

*For the revelation awaits an appointed time; it speaks of the end and will not prove false. Though it linger, wait for it; it will certainly come and will not delay.*
Habakkuk 2:3

 **Write out what God has revealed to you and thank Him for His faithfulness.**

# Search & Rescue

## Day 3: Blood, Sweat and Tears

Your homework today and tomorrow may feel disjointed from where we've spent our time earlier this week. But actually it's right where we need to be. We'll turn to a story in the Bible where two very different people went on a search.

Let's get started with this question: *How well do you handle interruptions?* Rate yourself on the **Irritation Scale** by circling your score:

| 0 | 1 | 2 | 3 | 4 | 5 |
|---|---|---|---|---|---|
| Not at all irritated Exasperated | | | Mildly Annoyed | | Extremely |

You probably said, "Well, it all depends on the situation…" I would agree.

Now imagine you have a life or death situation. You are bent on only one thing – getting help and getting it *fast*. Your heart is beating quickly, you're breathing heavy. You're sweating, mind racing with all of the "what if's" swirling around your head. You try desperately to keep your emotions under control. You keep telling yourself to hold it together. Others are depending on you. A lot rides on getting to where you're headed. Time is of the essence. You round the corner and you see it! It's the help you've been looking for…

And then the unthinkable happens.
    A delay.
        An interruption that steals precious time.

**What emotion(s) do you feel arise in this scenario? What score would you give yourself on the Irritation Scale now?**

The above scenario is taken from Scripture, although the emotions I've described are my own interpretation. **Read the story from Mark 5:21-43.** Keep your Bible open because we'll look at this passage together.

Notice any connecting points between the two supporting characters: Jairus and the woman? Jesus, of course, is the leading man in this story of hope. There's a treasure hidden in this story that is meant for you to unearth. Let's dig for it together. Let's pray for eyes to see:

> *God, show me Your truth! Give me eyes of faith to see what You want to do in my life. Give me the courage to respond in trust and obedience. In Jesus' Name. Amen.*

Let's start with Jairus, the synagogue ruler. He's the one searching for help in his family's life or death drama. He finds Jesus surrounded by a crowd who were thronging Him. Thronging is not a word we use in our vocabulary these days, but there's a strong chance you've experienced a good thronging. Have you ever attended a concert, major sporting event, or Black Friday Sale? If you've ever been in the middle of a packed crowd that's pushing and shoving, it can be a little frightening and nearly impossible to move against. But Jairus' desperation pushed him through that crowd until he got face to face with Jesus.

"*...and when he saw Jesus, he fell at His feet. He pleaded earnestly with Him, "My little daughter is dying. Please come and put Your hands on her so that she will be healed and live*" (Mark 5:23). This distraught father drops to his knees in front of Jesus and begs His help. "*So Jesus went with him*" (vs. 24).

I can only imagine Jairus' great relief to have Jesus by his side as they finally began making their way to his beloved daughter.

And then came the interruption.

Enter stage right: a woman who had been suffering from an issue of blood for the last 12 years.

Commentaries tell us that according to Jewish law, her husband could not touch her as long as she was hemorrhaging. Everything she touched was unclean. Whoever touched her would be unclean. Whoever touched anything she touched would be unclean. Therefore, she could not continue to live with her family, to prepare their food, wash their clothing, or care for their needs. Nor could she (according to Jewish Law) enter the place of worship as long as she was hemorrhaging. She was ceremonially unclean. For 12 years, she lived in the shadows.

**Can you relate? How long has your sexual past caused you to live in the shadows? Have you felt shut out or rejected by others?**




Like Jairus, she came in desperation. She risked being discovered, but that didn't stop her. Jesus was her only hope. She thought, "*If I just touch His clothes, I will be healed*" (Mark 5:28). The word "touch" in the Greek means to *grasp* or *clasp onto*. She didn't touch with her fingertips or brush against His clothing. Desperate times called for desperate measures. She *gripped* Jesus's clothes and "*...immediately her bleeding stopped and she felt in her body that she was healed*" (vs. 29).

Jesus asked, "*Who touched my clothes?*"

Mark 6:56 says "*wherever He went—into villages, towns or countryside—they placed the sick in the marketplaces. They begged Him to let them touch even the edge of His cloak, and all who touched it were healed.*" So what made this time different than the others? Why did Jesus want to call her out publicly?

**What do *you* think? Jot down your thoughts.**




**How did Jesus handle this interruption?**




Why would Jesus want to publicly call her out? Was it to condemn her for going against Jewish law? Did He intend to humiliate her?

*Then the woman, knowing what had happened to her, came and fell at his feet and, trembling with fear, told him the **whole** truth (vs. 33).* The whole truth included the long list of doctors who couldn't cure her, and the price she had paid—not only for ineffective medical treatment—but the emotional cost of living in the shadow of her family, community, and religious worship. She was *spent*—financially, physically, emotionally, relationally, and spiritually.

By His response to her, I'd say Jesus responded with compassion and grace—giving her what no doctor could. Not only did He send her away in peace, but with a tear-stained face glowing with gratitude.

Put yourself in this story. Picture your face hidden beneath that cloak to hide your identity from others. Picture your hand reaching out and grasping His clothes. He knows you're there. He feels your grasp of faith. He responds by giving you what you've come for. And you are **never** an interruption to Him.

As this woman's encounter was unfolding, it was also setting the stage to display God's power for Jairus. Certainly Jairus, who was standing at Jesus' side, had heard the woman's tearful story. So what about him? Why the delay in his crisis?

*Was* it a delay? Or maybe a *divine pause*?

Maybe it was all a big set-up. Jesus, being the Son of God, knowing that Jairus' daughter had already died, had set the stage to give Jairus a ray of hope in the midst of his grief. Jairus, walking shoulder to shoulder with Jesus toward his home, would have been a witness to Christ's display of power by someone simply *touching* Him. The woman suffered for 12 years. Is it simply coincidence that Jairus's daughter was 12 years old? Doubtful.

The look in Jairus' eyes must have given him away because Jesus said, *"Don't be afraid; just believe"* (verse 36).

You know how the story ends. Jesus and Jairus arrive at the home amid a crowd of wailing, mourning people. Taking only three of His disciples and the young daughter's parents, they enter the room where she lay. Jesus says, *"Talitha koum,"* which in Aramaic means more literally, **"My little lamb, arise."**

Let's put ourselves in the cloak or sandals of these characters in the story, and see if we can hear more clearly what God may be saying to us.

- Can you relate to the woman who suffered for 12 years trying every remedy known to doctors? Have you been under the care of a doctor or therapist for years without relief? (Read verse 34). Jesus told the woman: _____
- Can you relate to the father seeking help for his daughter? Perhaps your child is facing traumatic circumstances and you are desperate for intervention. (Read verse 36). Jesus told the father: _____

- Can you relate to the young daughter on her deathbed? Have you faced sickness or abuse at a tender age? Have you felt as though you've been on an emotional deathbed since childhood? (Read verse 41). Jesus told the little girl: _____

**Which character can you most identify with and why?**




**What are you desperate for God to do?**




Jesus met each of them in their suffering, in their crisis of belief, and in their dark shadows. Neither one of these cast of characters was an interruption to Jesus. They were each His divine intent. And so are you.

God's touch on our lives has a domino effect on others. As He redeems your sexual past, He's also using it to raise up courage and faith in someone else. No accidents. No vain interruptions. *His* intention and design. And your story will be the very thing that offers a ray of hope in someone's dark hour.

So, Beloved...
    Believe.
        Arise, little lamb.
            And go in peace.

 **My "I Get It!" thought for today:**

## Search & Rescue

### Day 4: The Truth, the Whole Truth and Nothing but the Truth

Rick Warren, author of **THE PURPOSE DRIVEN LIFE**, says, *"The start of any healing in your life is revealing your hurt. If you want to get over your emotional hurts, you have to share them with somebody. There is no closure without disclosure."* In yesterday's lesson, we got an up-close look at the woman in Mark 5 who had an issue of blood. Hers is a story of the power of disclosure.

Although we know the outcome of both Jairus and this woman, let's linger awhile and reflect on her emotions as described in Scripture.

> *And the woman, though she was afraid and trembling, aware of what had happened to her, came and fell down before Him and told Him the whole truth.* Mark 5:33 AMP

The *whole truth* can be very scary! This woman, Scripture says, was **alarmed, frightened, and trembled** with fear. On her knees before Jesus, her posture of humility begged for mercy and understanding. She came clean and *became* clean.

And so it is with us. The Lord invites us to tell Him the whole truth so that we can be made whole. It starts with being honest about our past.

> **Let's pray:** *Father, even though I may be frightened and trembling, I will trust You in this process. Take my little bit of courage and begin to set my heart and mind free from my past. In Jesus' Name. Amen.*

Today you're going to start working on your story. If you're doing this study as a group, be prepared to share it with the group. If you're doing this study on your own, be sure to share your story with a trusted friend, counselor, mentor, or pastor. This is a crucial step in your healing process.

Sharing your story is not about airing your dirty laundry. Rather, it's about releasing the hold of pain and shame in your life so that you can walk with Christ unhindered. Sharing our secrets can leave us feeling vulnerable, but I promise you that you will feel a sense of relief and freedom.

Exposing the lies and sin of our sexual past will bring into the light what has been hidden in the darkness and break the power of the secret. When we believe the lie that there's just too much to be forgiven, it gives power to the stronghold of lies. Your enemy, Satan, wants you to believe your pain and shame are *too much* to be forgiven, too much for anyone to hear. He will encourage you to keep stuffing and hiding it. Pretty soon we **believe** the lie and we'll do anything to keep it from being discovered, including lying, denial—you name it. We exert a lot of energy to keep those secrets covered up. Letting go can be scary, but unless we dare to open that cell door, we cannot be free.

There's a saying that goes, "You're as sick as your deepest secret." Look up and write out the following verses, noting how they relate to the above statement:

**James 5:16**

**John 8:31-32**

**Guidelines for sharing your story.**[8]
1. **Write out your story.** Do not "wing it." Writing it out will cause you to think of important details that you may otherwise miss.
2. **Pray and ask God to guide you and to remind you of important details of your story.** As you write, the Spirit of God will begin to reveal truth and lies. Be patient in the process. Grieve your losses.
3. **Use the following questions to guide you as you write your story:**
    - Share your first memory of being *exposed* to sex. How old were you? What happened? Who was involved? Where did it happen? How did it happen?
    - Share about your first sexual *experience*. How old were you? What happened? Who was involved? Where did it happen? Was it against your will? Were you a willing partner? Include any other significant details.
    - As you think back to that first experience, what were your thoughts and emotions at that time?
    - How was your life impacted by that first sexual experience? What kinds of choices did you make after that? Did you engage in risky behaviors? Did your attitudes about men or women change after that?
    - What are some of the consequences that you are dealing with today as a result of your sexual past?

**How did Jesus respond to the woman after she *"told him everything?"* Write out Mark 5:34:**

We see that Jesus is moved with compassion when we bring to Him the truth, the whole truth, and nothing but the truth. In faith, this woman came to Jesus for physical healing and went away with *much*, much more. Her physical healing paved the way for her broken, non-existent relationships to be restored. No longer unclean, she was now free to be a daughter, sister, wife, and mother. No longer isolated, even her worship was restored as she was now free to worship with her family and community. And if her physical healing brought about relational and spiritual restoration, what do you think it did for her emotional well-being? My guess is she was the loudest one singing in the choir on the Sabbath!

Bringing the truth, the whole truth, and nothing but the truth of your past to Jesus positions you for peace and freedom that you may have only dreamed about. Well done, Beloved.

 My "I Get It!" thought for today:

## Search & Rescue

### *Day 5: Search and Rescue*

Several years ago, my husband took a job with an out-of-state company because of the economy. That job, which he thought would be "six months tops" lasted more than two-and-a-half years. Due to the nature of his work schedule and driving distance, he made it home one or two days a month. Our children were very young, making the time away devastatingly painful for all of us. I felt like a single mom doing all of the parenting myself, not to mention taking care of our home and all that goes with it. And did I mention that I worked full time? I was lonely. My husband was lonely. The kids missed their Daddy. And Mommy cried and yelled a lot. Life was not like I thought it was supposed to be.

One day my dearest friend Kim called with a plan. She invited me on a personal retreat. What woman wouldn't jump on that? Except she wasn't going *with* me; I was going *alone*. Just me. She intended to pick up the kids Sunday morning and take them to church and lunch afterward. My instructions were to pack my Bible, journal, and a pen. Nothing else. When she came to my door, she had a lawn chair, blanket, and a tote filled with bottled water and snacks. She even handed me her iPod. She whisked off with my darlings while I considered a park or lake where I could seek God's face.

It was March. In Ohio March is cold and drab. Spring hadn't yet sprung, and that meant beauty was going to be very limited. I found a spot at a nearby lake, and I think I cried, complained and grumbled my way through the first half of my precious me-time. Finally, the sniffling stopped, and I got quiet before the Lord. I took inventory of where I had made "my spot." The edge of the lake was littered with debris, and there was a lot of overgrowth. Walking a short distance, I saw more of the same. I copped an attitude. I wanted to be surrounded by beauty, but I didn't see *anything* beautiful. Then I heard the quiet whisper of the Holy Spirit say to me, *"Look for the redeeming qualities."* I looked hard, but all I saw were overgrown weeds, downed branches, and litter.

I walked back to my spot and sat down. I looked across the lake and fixed my gaze on a beautiful home with a clean, neatly landscaped lawn. Pretty surprising considering it was March. I looked longingly at that home and wished I could be sitting on their dock where things looked well-kept and beautiful—not where I was sitting, among ugly debris. Again, God's Spirit whispered to me, *"It's beautiful there because someone is tending to it. And I am tending to you."* He wasn't harsh or accusing. He was gentle. And it made me feel *seen. Noticed. Loved.*

Why this random snapshot of my life? What significance did this have regarding my sexual past? Nothing. Well, not exactly. But it had much to do with my identity, my Search, and God's willingness to tend to the areas that still need to be cleaned up after a harsh winter of cold, damaging lies I've believed.

God didn't beckon me to the beautiful side of the lake so He could talk to me. Nor did He wait until my attitude was better. He met me right where I was, among the litter and muck. Whether we realize it now or not, the muck has a redemptive quality to it. God is committed to revealing it because He is the only one who can give us eyes to see beyond our circumstances. It might take years before we see its beauty, but He will patiently reveal it.

> Let's pray: *Lord, I'm going to believe and trust that You will complete the work You start in me and never abandon me. I'm not a project to be worked on, but a person that You love without conditions. Thank You for seeing me as worthy of Your attention. In Jesus' Name. Amen.*

Can you relate to being in a rut as I was? Do your relationships mirror the overgrown, littered lake edge I was sitting beside? Do you believe you deserve to sit in the muck because of your life choices? Do you believe God can (and will) redeem the mess of your past? Explain.

Your heavenly Father loves without strings attached. He searches the far country for the prodigal. He rescues from bondage. Yes, He is *good*. Oh taste and see that the Lord is good (Psalm 34:8).

**While it is true that God searches and pursues us, there is tremendous reward for those who seek after *Him*. Write out each verse and underline the promise:**

**Deuteronomy 4:29**

**Psalm 34:4**

**Psalm 9:10**

**Jeremiah 29:13**

**Write out the following verses and note the condition of the sheep or "the lost" and God's response to their need.**

**Ezekiel 34:6**

**Ezekiel 34:8**

**Ezekiel 34:11**

**Luke 19:10**

On social media, I came across a story (and photo) of a sheep that had gotten separated from the flock and was found in a faraway cave in the mountains six years later. I don't know if the story was true or not but the picture of that sheep sure told a tale! The wool had grown so thick and long one could barely see its eyes. Surely eating, walking, and climbing were a chore. Finally, the sheep was discovered by a shepherd who took the sheep, sheared its thick wool, and cared for it. I can only imagine how relieved the sheep was to be discovered and cared for after such a long time on its own, vulnerable to the elements, predators, and its own limitations.

Jesus is described in 1 Peter 5:4 as our Chief Shepherd. He is committed to your search and rescue, to your care, and to your healing. In Him alone can all our needs be met. We can trust Him with our past, our present, and our future. We can trust Him to redeem the ugly parts of our past—in His timing. He is patient and will never stop tending to us. Keep trusting. Be obedient to each step He asks you to take. It will not be in vain.

 **My "I Get It!" thought for today:**

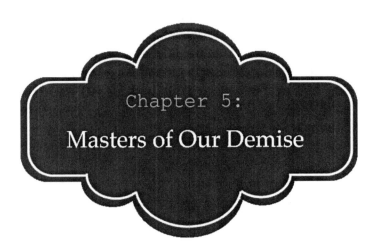

Chapter 5:
Masters of Our Demise

# Masters of Our Demise

*Day 1: The Wholeness of Holiness*

God calls us to share in His holiness: *"Be holy because I, the Lord your God, am holy"* (Leviticus 19:2). I once thought holiness was a nebulous concept—even downright *un*attainable. It's easy for God to be holy because He's GOD. But I'm just me, and I have a fairly good reputation for making messes.

God wouldn't tell us to be holy if it were not possible to do so. After closely examining the book of Leviticus and other verses throughout Scripture, I saw for myself that God plainly outlines holy and unholy behavior. In other words, God sees some things clearly as black and white. So get ready for some discussions this week on topics like pornography, emotional affairs, masturbation, and more! Does God really have an opinion on them? You might be surprised at what you learn. God wants us to live in the radiant Light of His holiness because holiness brings *wholeness*.

> **Let's pray:** *Father, teach me. Help me to desire holiness. Shine Your radiant light into the corners of my heart and mind and show me Your ways. In Jesus' Name. Amen.*

To get started, take a quick true or false quiz on state laws. Circle True or False for each statement below:

| State Laws: Right or Ridiculous? | | |
|---|---|---|
| In Missouri, it is illegal to drive with an uncaged bear. | True | False |
| In Wisconsin, it is illegal to serve butter substitutes in State prisons. | True | False |
| In South Carolina, you must be 18 years of age to play pinball. | True | False |
| In North Carolina, bingo games can't last more than 5 hours. | True | False |
| In Connecticut, it's illegal to walk across a street on your hands. | True | False |
| In Arizona, hunting camels is prohibited. | True | False |

How do you think you did? If you answered ***true*** to each of the above laws, you are correct. At one time, there was probably good reason for each of these laws to make the books. But over time these "rational" laws became nothing short of ridiculous.

*Unbound*

**If I asked you to describe the book of Leviticus (the 3rd book of the Old Testament) using only a few words or a short phrase, what would you say? Fill in the following blank:** _____

At first glance some may use the words *boring, rules,* or *laws* to describe the book of Leviticus. Unlike some of the ridiculous state laws we looked at above, we must remember that **all** Scripture is God-breathed (2 Tim. 3:16) and therefore useful (and relevant) to us today. While Leviticus cites some strange civil rules for handling food and addressing disease and sex, we can see God's heart toward mankind to protect His people from sickness and disease. In short, Leviticus is a guidebook for holy living.

**Write your own definition of what it means to be holy:** _____

Holiness is mentioned more times (152 to be exact) in Leviticus than in any other book of the Bible. Why was it so important? What was God trying to teach His people?

Holiness describes God Himself: *"Be holy because I, the Lord your God, am holy" (Lev. 19:2).*

> **Vine's Expository Dictionary**
> **Holy**: *It is predicted of God, as the absolutely Holy One in His purity, majesty and glory*
> Synonyms: sacred, set apart, pure, clean

In the book of Exodus, God had removed (or delivered) His people from Egypt; in Leviticus, He was removing Egypt from His people. God wanted His people to be different from the nations around them. From the foods they ate, to their sexual practices and pattern of worship, God called them to be set apart from those around them. It would require forsaking deeply rooted customs and beliefs and adopting a new standard—*a new identity* as God's chosen people. The call of every believer today is the same as it was long ago.

**Write out the following verses:**

**2 Corinthians 6:17**



**John 15:19**



Just as God was removing Egypt (its culture and sinful customs) from His people, God wants us to partner with Him to remove the world from our lives so that we (as Believers) look different from those around us.

Look up the following verses and write out the main thought of each verse:

1 John 2:16

Ephesians 2:1-3

**According to these verses, what type of behavior or attitude is God calling us to reject?**

We are clearly told to reject *gratifying* the cravings of the flesh or lust of the flesh, as well as the lust of the eyes and the pride of life. Let's look a little deeper into what these things mean:

- **Lust, desire or craving of the flesh**: *a desire or longing for what is forbidden; what one wishes or has determined shall be done.*

    **Have you indulged in a forbidden romance with a married man/woman? If not, have you *longed for* a romance with a certain married man/woman (in your mind or heart)? In what ways have you indulged or longed for any sexual relationship outside of marriage?**

- **Lust of the eyes**: *desire excited by seeing. Includes envy.*

    **Have you been aroused with sexual desire by what you've seen in secular or pornographic magazines or movies? Have you taken second and third looks at scantily clothed men/women because you liked what you saw? Have you dressed seductively to attract attention from others? Explain.**

- **Pride of life**: *braggart talk. An insolent and empty assurance, which trusts in its own power and resources and shamefully despises and violates divine laws and human rights. An impious and empty presumption which trusts in the stability of earthly things.*

    **Examine your attitudes about your past sexual indiscretions. Were you brazen or unashamed by your sexual relationships or infidelities?**

In our feel-good, anything-goes culture, we might think that real sexual freedom is having what we want, who we want, when and how we want it.

No limits.
    No restrictions.
        No commitments.

We may reason:
    *"We just couldn't help ourselves."*
        *"Things just happened."*
            *"I'm not hurting anyone."*

My guess is that if you're reading this book, you've already discovered those simply aren't true. Gratifying our lusts has hurt our heart and our emotions. We are broken. However, following God's ways **will** bring us freedom. Our wholeness is found in holiness.

 **My "I Get It!" thought for today:**

## Masters of Our Demise

### Day 2: God's No-Fly Zone

A no-fly zone is a territory over which aircraft are not permitted to fly. These zones are usually set up in a military context and ban military aircraft of a belligerent nation from operating in the region. Aircraft that break the no-fly zone risk *serious* consequences.

Today we'll examine **God's No-Fly Zone** for sexual activity. Like military no-fly zones, God's No-Fly Zone outlines sexual "territories" that we are not to cross. These restricted areas are created to protect us against serious consequences – not the least of these is sinning against a holy God.

> **Let's pray:** *Father, give me ears to hear and a heart to obey Your Laws. Realign my attitudes and views in the places where I've crossed sacred boundaries. I want to honor You in my public and private life. In Jesus' Name. Amen.*

God established laws (or boundaries) in order to protect His people. Acting outside of His established laws carry physical, relational, emotional, and spiritual consequences.

**Read Psalm 19:7-12.**

| **List nine attributes of God's laws, statutes or commands:** | **List six benefits of trusting God's precepts or laws:** |
|---|---|
| _____ | _____ |
| _____ | _____ |
| _____ | _____ |
| _____ | _____ |
| _____ | _____ |
| _____ | _____ |
| _____ | |
| _____ | |
| _____ | |

In Psalm 19:12a David says, *"Who can discern his errors?"* David knew his sins were illumined in the light of God's precepts. Likewise, we cannot discern the darkness of our sin without the light of God's commands or boundaries. God gives many clear safeguards for holy living when it comes to sex.

Following is a clear list of No-Fly, Absolutely-Not commands that are found in Scripture.[1]

| ADULTERY | Having sex with the spouse of another person. (Can be mental, physical or spiritual.)<br>**Exodus 20:14, Leviticus 20:10, Matthew 5:27-28, Ezekiel 23:37** |
|---|---|
| FORNICATION | Illicit sexual intercourse (includes adultery, homosexuality, lesbianism, intercourse with animals, intercourse with close relatives, etc.)<br>**Leviticus 18, Matthew 15:19, Mark 7:21** |
| HOMOSEXUALITY | To lie (of sexual relations) with a man as one lies with a woman.<br>**Leviticus 18:22, Romans 1:27** |
| IMPURITY | In a moral sense: the impurity of lustful, luxurious, decadent, shameless living.<br>**Numbers 5:12-13, Galatians 5:19** |
| INCEST | Sexual relations with a close relative.<br>**Leviticus 18:6-18, 1 Corinthians 5:1** |
| LUSTFUL PASSION | Desire, craving, longing, desire for what is forbidden; unbridled lust, excess, licentiousness, wantonness, outrageousness, shamelessness, insolence (includes filthy words, indecent bodily movements, immoral handling of males and females).<br>**Mark 7:21-22, Galatians 5:19, 1 Peter 4:3** |
| OBSCENITY | Includes facetiousness, crude jokes, low jesting, rude and abusive language, vulgarity, raunchiness, profanity, innuendos.<br>**Ephesians 4:29, Ephesians 5:4** |
| ORGIES | Sexual encounters involving many people.<br>**Galatians 5:21, 1 Peter 4:3** |
| PROSTITUTION | To profane, defile, pollute, desecrate oneself (ritually or sexually); to make common, to violate the honor of.<br>**Leviticus 19:29, Proverbs 7:4-27** |
| SODOMY | Unnatural sexual intercourse especially of one man with another or of a human being with an animal. Men lying with men.<br>**Leviticus 18:22-23; Romans 1:26** |

*Compiled by Dr. Joseph Dillow/Adapted for this book.*

Take the time to look up the Scriptures on the chart and read them for yourselves. Does God give clear boundaries for holy and unholy sex? What did God show you about His No-Fly Zone? Are you surprised by anything?

 My "I GET IT!" thought for today:

*Masters of Our Demise*

*Day 3: Black, White, and Shades of Gray*

God's No-Fly Zone of sexual conduct covers the black and white issues. Are **all** sexual issues black and white? We will discover that some issues definitely fall into the gray scale. Can we really know what God thinks about the shades of gray?

**Let's pray:** *Lord, sometimes I can be fooled by shades of gray—things that seem okay to me. Show me any offensive practices in my life that are not pleasing to You. Let the light of Your Word guide my steps and keep me from stumbling (Psalm 119:105). In Jesus' Name. Amen.*

**Write out the following verses:**

I Corinthians 6:12


I Corinthians 10:23-24


If something falls into God's No-Fly Zone, we don't have to search any further. We have a clear answer. But what about the shades of gray? I believe we can know what God thinks about gray areas too. From the book **PULLING BACK THE SHADES**, authors Dr. Juli Slattery and Dannah Gresh provide some guidelines to ask ourselves based on 1 Corinthians 6:12, 10:23-24: [2]

- **Is this beneficial?** Is it good for me? My husband? Is it good for our marriage?
- **Does it master me?** Can it be habit-forming or addictive?
- **Is it constructive?** Does it help me grow mature? Does it build our marriage?
- **Is it loving?** Does this action show love toward others or is it selfish?

*Pornography*

Surprised to see pornography on the Gray List? To some, pornography is clearly wrong. But for others, the issue is clear as mud. In addition, being advised by those in authority to "spice things up" by viewing pornography in your marriage can cause further confusion.

Chances are you have been exposed to some form of pornography in your adolescence—if not as a child. Most likely we stumbled upon it because of someone else. Perhaps pornography is not an issue that you're currently struggling with. But is the *ghost* of pornography still haunting you?

Pornography is not just a *he* problem, but a *she* problem, too. Statistics show that more than one-third of pornography viewers are women. Another source concluded that 68 percent of Christian women who were surveyed say they admit to watching pornography frequently. And 55 percent admitted that watching pornography felt out of control.[3] In addition, there are approximately 68 *million* search engine requests for pornography—*daily*—by both men and women.[4]

Pornography is progressive. Its influence is gradual; the more you see it, the more you want it. When viewing porn, sexual arousal can be intense. Like any 'high' your body will crave another hit. This is scientifically proven. Dopamine is the chemical in your brain that is released every time you experience pleasure. If it feels good, we want to do it *again and again*. From the book **HOOKED,** by Drs. Joe McIlhaney, Jr., and Freda Bush, *"Dopamine is values-neutral. In other words, it's an involuntary response that cannot tell right from wrong, or beneficial from harmful—it rewards all kinds of behavior without distinction."*[5] This is how something destructive can become an addiction.

Pornography may deliver sexual arousal, but it will never deliver sexual *intimacy*. Seeking sexual fulfillment through pornography will inevitably leave you unsatisfied. For starters, it will subtly affect the way we view the sexes. Essentially, women lose their relational value to men and are viewed as only sexual objects. (Men are objectified too.) The effects are especially obvious in marriage relationships when a spouse must compete with the hundreds of anonymous "others" who are now in their bed.

• • •

### Sarah's story: Just the Three of Us

"I planned a boudoir photo shoot as a gift for my husband. I carefully selected the photographer—the sister of a close friend. Before committing to the project, I stressed my need for confidentiality. As a professional, I certainly didn't want anything resurfacing to harm my reputation or career. She assured me it would be "just between the three of us." That statement caused a check in my spirit but I brushed it off. Coincidentally, I just happened to be working through a Bible study to heal from my sexual past. I was 24 hours away from the photo shoot and God used these clarifying questions to show me that even though this was a gift to my husband, it involved someone else—the photographer—and in God's eyes it was wrong. I thank Him for showing me the truth!"

• • •

Let's use our guiding questions to discern if pornography is a black and white issue, or if it falls into the gray area:
1. **Is pornography forbidden in Scripture?** Review the items listed in God's No-Fly Zone from yesterday's homework. Write them here.

2. **Is it beneficial to me and/or my marriage?** List at least 3 ways that support your answer:

3. **Does it master me?**

4. **Is it constructive? Is it loving?**

It's safe to say that we can officially move pornography from our Shades of Gray List to something that God sees as black and white.

**In what ways have you been affected by pornography in your past? Is it still an issue for you?**

**What "needs" did pornography provide for you?**

**Whether pornography is a past or present struggle, there are likely emotional and spiritual issues that need to be addressed. Is it loneliness? Feeling disconnected, angry, or depressed?**

*Sexting*

Sexting is electronically sending nude, sexually suggestive or explicit photos, videos, or messages. Sexting is more common among teens, but surprisingly, about 20 percent of young adults send sexts. According to a National Campaign survey for 20- to 26-year-olds, this could be as high as 33 percent.[6] (Some findings show up to 46 percent.) Sexting is becoming more prevalent among older generations too. One study revealed 1 out of 10 Baby Boomers admitted to sending or receiving explicit photos. The largest number of males who sext are between 18—34, while women who sext tend to be older, in the 35—44 year-old range. One woman touting the benefits of sexting commented, *"It's smart to squeeze in a little sexting foreplay before dating. The world is online now and so is dating. People like to window shop."*[7]

Like pornography, most people see sexting as a black and white issue, rather than a shade of gray. And yet others have never considered that sexting is a form of pornography. Use our key questions to find out the answer.

1. **Is it forbidden in Scripture? (Review God's No-Fly Zone)**

2. **Is it beneficial?**

3. **Is it habit-forming?**

4. Is it constructive? Is it loving?

How has sexting influenced your sexual activity?

Do you consider sexting to be a form of intimacy? Why or why not?

 Write your "I Get It!" thought for today:

## Masters of Our Demise

### Day 4: More Shades of Gray

Today we're going to look at more shades of gray: emotional affairs and masturbation.

Most women are open to discussing porn issues in their past, but they are unusually quiet when it comes to the topic masturbation. Perhaps you see no big deal about emotional affairs or masturbation. *"They're harmless,"* you reason. *"It's a personal thing. I'm not hurting anyone."*

> **Let's pray:** *Lord, I admit I'm uncomfortable looking at these shades of gray. Search my heart and expose the cravings of my soul—those things that keep me stuck, stumbling, or trapped in negative patterns. I need Your truth to set me free. In Jesus' Name. Amen.*

### Emotional Affairs

An emotional affair is when one partner goes outside the primary relationship to get his or her emotional needs met. It all starts out innocently enough...
Frequent lunch dates.
  Grabbing drinks after work.
    Texting one another a little too much.
      Searching social media sites for an old high school flame.

With today's technology, it's easier than ever to start something with *any*one. It doesn't matter if they live in another city or country, if you're already acquainted with them or you've never met them in person. It's easy to find someone in online chat rooms, internet dating sites, etc., and to begin the intoxicating ritual of emails and text messages that lead to *something*. It may not be physical, but it's not completely innocent either.

Like a physical affair, emotional affairs are secretive. They drain the primary relationship of authentic intimacy and vulnerability. Once the emotional connection is there, the physical part becomes easier to engage in. Fantasizing can pave the way for a sexual relationship.

Monika Lewis, in an article written for Focus on the Family, identifies a number of factors that can lead to having an emotional affair:[8]

- You share personal thoughts or stories with someone of the opposite sex
- You feel greater emotional intimacy with him/her than you do with your spouse
- You start comparing him/her to your spouse and begin listing why your spouse doesn't add up
- You long for, and look forward to, your next contact or conversation
- You start changing your normal routine or duties to spend more time with him/her
- You feel the need to keep conversations or activities involving him/her a secret from your spouse

> • • •
>
> **Jennifer's story: Feed My Ego**
>
> "I had been in a relationship for a few years. I wanted a marriage commitment, but my boyfriend was non-committal. Over time, I found myself shutting down emotionally. There was a man at work—a married man—that began feeding my ego. He told me how pretty I was and made excuses to call me. I was consumed with thoughts about him and started fantasizing about him. Having lunch with him seemed so innocent. After a while, those lunches led to a physical affair."
>
> • • •

- You fantasize about spending time with, getting to know, or sharing a life with him/her
- You spend significant time alone with him/her

Again, let's look at emotional affairs against our guiding questions:

1. **Is it forbidden in Scripture?** Review the items listed in God's No-Fly Zone.

2. **Is it beneficial to me and/or my marriage?**

3. **Does it master me?**

4. **Is it constructive? Is it loving?**

Answering the above questions truthfully gives clarity to emotional affairs: they are dangerous and not at all beneficial.

## *Masturbation*

Masturbation is not specifically mentioned in the Bible. So is it a sin or not? Since it's not clearly mentioned, we have added it to our gray list.

Like pornography, masturbation is not just a *he* thing, but a *she* thing too. Many struggle with this issue, but few actually talk about it. While masturbation remains a taboo subject, we're going to open up the closet door and shed some light on this secretive issue.

Masturbation is *self*-pleasuring to achieve sexual climax, whether you're married or not. For the purpose of our discussion, we are not including masturbation or mutual masturbation between a husband and wife during lovemaking.

Let's look at how masturbation affects the whole person: physically, emotionally, and spiritually. Physically, both sexes would agree that masturbating produces a more intense climax than is achieved through sexual intercourse.

Masturbation trains us to find pleasure in a specific way. If we get used to experiencing pleasure in our own way, we won't go to our husband to fill that need. This is where masturbation can threaten our emotional intimacy with our husband or future spouse. We go through the motions of lovemaking and feel frustrated because we can't achieve orgasm without masturbating. Instead of communicating with our husband and helping him to learn how to pleasure us, our DIY (do-it-yourself) mentality reasons that we can "take care of things ourselves later." Communication and mutual discovery are what develop emotional bonds in lovemaking.

Masturbation is a strong conditioner of behavior. Earlier we talked about the pleasure center of the brain that releases dopamine. It is values-neutral, meaning it wants to repeat that good feeling, regardless of whether it's a positive or negative action. When we experience sexual release, whatever we're fantasizing or fixating on becomes our trigger. What's arousing us? *Who's* arousing us? What are we watching? Pornography? R-rated movies? Smutty TV? What are we reading? Let's be honest: our minds go *somewhere* when we masturbate. And that somewhere can lead us into dangerous territory.

Masturbation weakens our determination to remain sexually pure within marriage *and* outside of marriage. Within marriage, because of the many reasons we've already stated. As a single, if we're unable to control our passions when we're alone, how will we do in a romantic relationship?

So what have you concluded about masturbation? Although we don't see definite Scriptural evidence, Louis McBurney, in an article for **Today's Christian Woman**, says, *"Masturbation under some circumstances could be sin. If masturbation is used as a way to deny sex to your spouse, that would be destructive and go against the 1 Corinthians 7 principles described by (the Apostle) Paul. If masturbation is accompanied by fantasies of extra-marital relations, it may fit with Jesus' definition of lust in Matthew 5."*[9]

> **Linda's story: Desire for True Intimacy**
>
> "It was always so much easier to take care of my needs myself. After all, I knew my body best and how to achieve orgasm. However, the closer I grew in the Lord, the more I desired true intimacy with my husband. The Lord showed me that my take-care-of-myself mentality was robbing my marriage of the beautiful intimacy that the Lord wanted to bless us with. I have not masturbated for nearly two years now. I'm finding that my husband can satisfy me and our intimacy is growing with each new encounter."

Let's look at masturbation against the scale of our key questions.

1. **Is it forbidden in Scripture?**



2. **Is it beneficial to me and/or my marriage?**



3. **Does it master me?**



4. **Is it constructive? Is it loving?**



We see that masturbation is not beneficial to ourselves or to the marriage relationship when we DIY. As we conclude today's homework, let's take a look at the following scripture:

**Write out Matthew 5:29**




In Matthew 5, Jesus advises us how to deal with temptation. *Any* temptation. His strong warning includes fantasy, pornography, online relationships, and erotica. Dr. Juli Slattery, in an article for **Today's Christian Woman** titled "**Guidelines for Christian Sex**" writes: *(Jesus') message is clear: get rid of whatever causes you to sin in your heart. If it is a portal for temptation, get rid of the iPhone, satellite TV, or your Facebook account. Cut off the relationship that is tempting you. Throw out the mommy porn. Stop flirting with anything that causes you to think, lust or fantasize about someone other than your spouse."*[10]

Regardless of the bait, the end result is the same. Sin will draw us somewhere we really don't want to go. Temptation is the sizzle of excitement. The aftermath of sin is guilt, shame, and self-loathing.

Embrace the tools you've learned for discerning gray-area issues so you can live a guilt-free, holy life that bring wholeness.

 **My "I Get It!" thought for today:**

## Masters of our Demise

### Day 5: Upholding Holiness

We started this week looking at holiness that leads to wholeness. When God removed His people Israel from Egypt, the work was just beginning. What followed was a lifetime of removing Egypt from their lives—exchanging Egyptian ways of living and thinking for God's ways. This included sexual conduct and practices, among others things.

After your conversion to Christ, the sanctifying process had just begun. Pursuing after God will require you to exchange—or surrender—old ways of living and patterns of thinking. The process of breaking free from these strong tethers can be difficult, but they are not impossible with God's Spirit living in you. It's something we must learn to do if we are to be holy and whole.

> **Let's pray:** *Father, I find myself in a mental rut at times. Old desires are hard to break free from. Cut off the ties that bind and give me a heart to follow Your ways. Help me to want to carve out a new path that leads to wholeness. In Jesus' Name. Amen.*

Forsaking old ways and learning new patterns of behavior involves our heart and mind. Jesus taught in Matthew 15 that we are not defiled by what we touch or eat, but rather by the words we speak from the heart. *"For out of the heart come evil thoughts—murder, adultery, sexual immorality, theft, false testimony, slander"* (Matt. 5:18). We have a **heart** problem.

Ephesians 2:2-3 states, *"when you followed the ways of this world"* we were clearly *"gratifying the cravings of our flesh.* The KJV adds, *"...and of the mind."* Not only do we have a heart problem, but we also have a problem with our **mind**—what we think about.

**According to the above verses, where does sin originate?**

**Write out Romans 12:2**

**The "pattern of this world" refers to what our culture endorses as good and right. What does the "pattern of this world" say about the following things? How do the world's views and God's views differ? Have you adopted some of the same views as the world?**

|  | The World's View on... | God's View on... |
|---|---|---|
| **ABORTION** | | |
| **CASUAL SEX/ HOOKING UP** | | |
| **FRIENDS WITH BENEFITS** | | |
| **LIVING TOGETHER** | | |
| **MARRIAGE** | | |

God may be showing you areas in your life that need to be addressed. If so, respond to His nudging and draw near to Him. Here are some basic steps:

1. **ACKNOWLEDGE**

    Acknowledge the gap that exists between God's views and your views/practices regarding your sexual past or present.

    *Fools make fun of guilt, but the godly acknowledge it and seek reconciliation.* Proverbs 14:9 NLT

2. **CONFESS**

    Acknowledging something is different from confessing it. We can acknowledge wrongful actions in our heart and mind yet continue those behaviors. Confession involves *action*: using our mouth and words to agree with God that a particular behavior is sin. We can't *be* clean without *coming* clean.

    *If we confess our sins, He is faithful and just and will forgive us our sins
    and purify us from all unrighteousness.*
    1 John 1:9

3. **REPENT**

    Repenting is similar to confession in that it involves action, but it goes much deeper than words. Repentance is having a change of mind about our sin. This change of mind involves both a turning *from* sin and a turning *to* God.

    *In the same way, I tell you, there is rejoicing in the presence of the
    angels of God over one sinner who repents.*
    Luke 15:10

4. **WALKING IT OUT: UPHOLDING HOLINESS**
It can be hard to live differently than those around us. Everywhere we turn, we are barraged with opposing views and sensual messages. We can honor God and live free despite the temptations around us.

*Just as you used to offer yourselves as slaves to impurity and to ever-increasing wickedness, so now offer yourselves as slaves to righteousness leading to holiness.* Romans 6:19b

**To be victorious over temptations in our lives, we must S.E.E.K God:**

***S —Submit to God:*** *Submit yourselves, then, to God. Resist the devil, and he will flee from you* (James 4:7). We are told to do two things: First, we are told to submit. Then we are to resist. When we fall into temptation it is because we either resist God and submit to the enemy or we try to resist temptation in our own strength. But God promises that if we submit to Him **first**, *then* resist the devil, there will be some action all right. The devil will be fleeing! We need His power to overcome the devil and temptation. Jesus modeled this for us in Matthew 4.
***E —Examine Thoughts:*** *"We demolish arguments and every pretension that sets itself up against the knowledge of God, and we take captive every thought to make it obedient to Christ"*
(2 Corinthians 10:5). What are we thinking about? Do we allow our mind to wander off into no-good places? Tempting thoughts will come. That's not the sin. Acting upon those thoughts is sin. We have the power to control what we dwell on. When negative or tempting thoughts come, take up your weapon and demolish every argument and pretension that opposes the Lord. We will recognize the thoughts that oppose God as we get a steady diet of God's Word. Knowing His truth makes us more prepared to handle the "junk food" that the world dishes out. A steady diet of cultural messages that contradict God's Word will make it harder to discern truth and overcome temptations.
***E—Exercise Discernment:*** *"Do not be misled: Bad company corrupts good character"* (1 Corinthians 15:33). Be discerning about the company you keep. Do you hang out with people of questionable character? Are you putting yourself in tempting situations? If you're single and dating, don't invite him into your apartment. If you're married, don't have lunch alone with a man who is not your husband. If you're struggling with pornography, don't take your laptop or tablet on out-of-town business. Have some accountability. Give permission to a trusted friend or counselor to ask you the tough questions about your activities to keep you on track.
***K—Keep Praying!*** If you fall, don't give up. While you're down, pull yourself to your knees and seek God's forgiveness. Acknowledge, confess, and repent. Then, get up and keep walking. God is right beside you on this journey of healing. He's encouraging your victory, cheering you on. He will never leave you or leave you where you are because...

*...He who began a good work in you will carry it on to completion*
*until the day of Christ Jesus.*
Philippians 1:6

**My "I GET IT!" thought for today:**

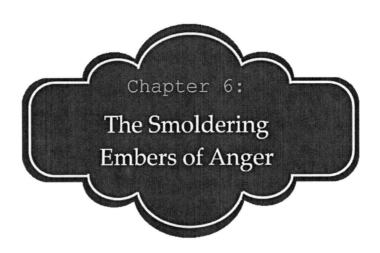

Chapter 6:
The Smoldering Embers of Anger

# The Smoldering Embers of Anger

*Day 1: The Danger of Smoldering Embers*

This week, we'll look at the emotion of anger and how we're dealing with it – *or how it's dealing with us.* Anger is synonymous with rage, wrath, fury, and indignation. Like heat, anger has many degrees, ranging from mild irritations to fiery explosions. Anger is an uncomfortable emotion because of its negative implications. Yet anger is common to every person. Although we know that in our *head*, we may identify this strong emotion as undesirable, destructive, and even sinful.

Denying the strength or existence of anger will only cause it to find other secondary outlets, as we'll discover. Do not fear lifting this scab from your wound. There are no Band-Aids in God's first-aid kit, Beloved. He is your Great Physician, and He alone is able to **heal** you.

> **Let's pray:** *Lord, looking at my anger seems like a pretty scary thing to me. Give me courage to press on and to look at things honestly. Show me how my anger has worked for me and against me. Teach me Your ways. In Jesus' Name. Amen.*

From the time you were just a little girl, more than likely, you learned to *be nice*. Repeated over and over throughout our childhood, the message becomes clear: *Good girls don't get angry. Anger is bad. Hide bad feelings.*

Such was the case in my personal life, although my parents never said it quite like that. Thankfully, neither of them had explosive tempers. I never ran in fear from their anger. In fact, my parents so rarely showed any outward expressions of anger that when they *did*, I remembered it!

I never thought I had any issues with anger until I reached my thirties. And then it seemed that everything made me mad! The anger I felt was very uncomfortable. My goodness, I was a *Christian*. A Christian who served in *ministry*. I served in my church. I'd gone on several mission trips. Christians aren't supposed to be angry people. To be honest, I thought that someone with an anger problem had a God-problem. When anger began to surface in my life over and over in ugly ways, Guilt and Shame would make me stuff it back down. It worked for a while until the next trigger. Then I would explode until I didn't recognize myself. Guilt and Shame coaxed me into stuffing it again – a little deeper this time. And the cycle would repeat itself. I'd cry out to God. I'd bargain with Him. Plead with Him. Nothing worked. I felt like there must be some flaw in me that couldn't be fixed.

I felt like a bad Christian.
    I felt like a fake.
        I felt hopeless.

During that destructive decade, I had already worked through an enormous amount of pain from my sexual past. That was done and over with. I couldn't trace my anger back to any particular person or event anymore. So what was going on? I tearfully confided in my closest friend about my struggle with anger and my explosive outbursts. I had kept it hidden from my husband. I was afraid to risk exposure and abandonment. Eventually I *did* share with my husband, and he extended understanding and grace. Although my outbursts were irregular, it took a decade of now-and-then explosive outbursts and self-destructive behaviors before I knew in my heart that I needed help. I cried out to God and pleaded with Him to expose my roots of anger, to teach me what to do and to heal me. I asked Him to help me expose what's been buried and to help me process through it. He did. Because I chose to get well, the pain of uncovering has been worth it.

**How about you? How much of a temper do you have? Ask yourself these kinds of questions:**
- *Do I suppress or hide my anger?*
- *Do I get irritated when someone gets in my way on or off the road?*
- *Do I get upset when my supervisor fails to give me credit where credit is due?*
- *Do I get upset when someone criticizes my appearance, my work, or my opinions?*
- *Do I get angry when someone takes advantage of me?*
- *Do I berate myself when I make a mistake or do poorly in front of others?*
- *Do I get upset with myself when I put off important things?*
- *Do I get angry with myself when I go against my better judgment or violate my own morals?*
- *Do I cry easily?*
- *Am I quick to shout or swear if I drop something or if anything goes wrong when doing simple tasks?*
- *Do I get overheated while waiting in lines even though I've got plenty of time to get served and be where I need to be next?*
- *Am I quick to get irritated with friends or family?*

**How did you do? Are you struggling with anger? Based on the previous questions, evaluate yourself on the scale below:**

| Rarely Angry | Occasionally Miffed | Regularly Riled | Rage-aholic |
|---|---|---|---|
| 0  1  2 | 3  4  5 | 6  7  8 | 9  10 |

**What triggers your anger? (Feelings, places, certain people, etc.)**

**How did your mother express anger? How did that make you feel?**

**How did your father express anger? How did that make you feel?**

**What kinds of messages did you receive as a child about anger? Was it okay to express anger?**

**How do you express your anger toward those closest to you? Strangers? Yourself?**

**How do you feel about the way you express anger?**

**Whether you were sexually violated or sexually promiscuous, what did you do with your anger? In what ways do/did you act out? Did you internalize your anger?**

Some may struggle with expressing anger because they believe "*Christian's aren't supposed to act that way*" or "*Good girls don't behave like that.*" So we get pretty good at stuffing it. And boy, can we look like we've got it all together. If we're not taught healthy ways to manage our anger, we're left burying it. What's to become of those smoldering embers? Do they eventually die out? Maybe. *But doubtful.*

Freud once compared anger to the smoke in an old-fashioned wood-burning stove. The normal outlet of smoke is up the chimney. However, if the chimney is blocked, the smoke will leak out of the stove in unintended ways—around the door, through the grates, etc.—choking everyone in the room.

Hidden anger gets buried within where it has the potential to undermine our sense of self and manifest in damaging ways—affecting our relationships and even our health. How can hidden anger rear its toxic head?

The items on the following checklist are signals that anger may be bottled up. Each symptom can be caused by things other than anger. (For instance, procrastination can be due to the fear of failure.) However, any manifestation should motivate us to look within, asking God to reveal any repressed anger.

## Hidden Anger Checklist [1]

*Physical Signs:*

_____ Grinding the teeth and/or clenched jaws, especially while sleeping
_____ Chronically stiff or sore neck or shoulder muscles
_____ Unintentional, habitual foot tapping or facial tics
_____ Knot in the stomach; stomach ulcers
_____ Tired more easily than usual
_____ Sleeping more than usual, maybe 12—14 hours a day
_____ Difficulty getting to sleep or sleeping through the night
_____ Waking up tired rather than feeling rested and refreshed
_____ Migraine headaches
_____ High blood pressure
_____ Arthritis
_____ Asthma
_____ Colitis
_____ Frequent colds

*Behavioral Signs:*
_____ Procrastination in the completion of imposed tasks
_____ Habitual lateness
_____ Sarcasm, cynicism, or flippancy in conversation
_____ Frequent sighing
_____ Over-politeness, constant cheerfulness, "grin and bear it" attitude
_____ Smiling while hurting
_____ Over-controlled monotone speaking voice
_____ Frequent, disturbing, or frightening dreams
_____ Boredom, apathy, loss of interest
_____ Excessive irritability over small things
_____ Rebuking yourself
_____ Yelling at others
_____ Gossiping
_____ Hitting others
_____ Breaking dishes or other objects
_____ Condescending to others
_____ Angry fantasies
_____ Chronic depression, feeling down for an extended period of time
_____ Addictions, self-destructive behavior, hurting yourself physically, significant weight gain, compulsive or binge-eating

God in all His goodness beckons us toward the path of healing and wholeness. He knows what you need and how to bring it about in your life. God knows your struggle, and He knows why it's there. He knows the things you've stuffed as a little child because you didn't know what to do with it. In your adolescence, He knows about the anger you turned inward because of the abuse you may have experienced. In your adulthood, perhaps those same habits—or strongholds—of exploding or turning inward have remained. God is able to teach you and bring you to a place of peace. You can trust Him.

**Write out Psalm 25:7-9 from the NLT and underline what God will do for those who go astray from His path.**

 **My "I Get It!" thought for today:**

## The Smoldering Embers of Anger

### Day 2: *Do you want to get well?*

Yesterday we discovered that hidden anger can make us sick. Not only can it show up in our physical bodies, but our actions may reveal smoldering embers beneath the surface. Under the right circumstances – or triggers – those embers can kick into a raging firestorm.

Today, we're going to look into the story of the invalid man in John 5. Scripture is relevant to us today. The styles and customs may change through the centuries, but the truths are timeless.

> **Let's pray:** *Father, I'm Yours. Nothing is hidden from You. I will quiet my heart before You. Send forth Your word and heal me. In Jesus' Name. Amen.*

**Read John 5:1-14**

This true account of an invalid man lying at the pool at Bethesda tells us that he was one among a great number of disabled people—the blind, lame, and paralyzed—who were waiting for the same thing: the stirring of the waters. The KJV adds, *"an angel went down at a certain season into the pool, and troubled the water: whosoever then first after the troubling of the water stepped in was made whole of whatsoever disease he had"* (vs. 4).

**What kind of people were waiting at the pool of water? What do they all have in common?**

**What special circumstances were required in order to be healed?**

We also learn that the man had been an invalid for 38 years. There's no mention that he was *born* an invalid. Additionally, Jesus' comment in verse 14 supports that the man's sickness happened later in life. After 38 years of a debilitating sickness, he had probably become accustomed to a new way of life; he found a new normal, so to speak. He may have lost all hope of ever being healed – that is, except for the stirring of the waters that happened *at a certain season*. It was a longshot, but it was all he had.

And then Jesus asks what seems to be a ridiculous question: *"Do you want to get well?"*

If that were me, I might have retorted, *"Are you kidding? Look at me! Look at everyone around me! What do you think?!"*

**So what *do* you think? Why would Jesus ask him such an obvious question?**

**How does the man answer Jesus?**

Did you catch the man's indirect answer to Jesus' simple question? The invalid gave an excuse, but Jesus responded with a command: "*Get up...and walk,*" and he was cured (vs. 9). The invalid was looking to the wrong person to make him whole. When we think we have no one, Jesus is our One and Only.

What about you? Do you *want* to be well? Where have you been looking for your healing? To what sources have you been running?

**There's a difference between wanting to be well and wanting to feel better. Explain the difference below.**

**Who or what have you been looking toward to make you feel better?**

**What excuses have you been making for staying stuck?**

**Read John 5:14 in the KJV**

We don't know the specific details of the man's condition, but we learn that it could have been connected to sin. In the Greek, Jesus used a combination of words when using the word *worse* to emphasize the seriousness of the matter. It speaks of a certain persons or things concerning which the writer either cannot or will not speak. In other words, Jesus dared not even say out loud what could happen if the man continued to sin.

A reckless life of drugs, alcohol abuse, and illicit sex can take a toll on one's health in obvious ways. But as we've already seen, the smoldering embers of hurt, unforgiveness, and anger can also wreak havoc on our physical bodies, as well as our souls. Stuffing it isn't working anymore, is it? Like that blocked chimney we talked about yesterday, those smoldering embers have now become a liability.

**So let's be honest before God. Picture yourself among the crowd of disabled people at the pool. In what ways has your sexual past left you feeling lame, blind, or paralyzed?**

If we want to be made well, then it will come with some work. It's time to unpack more emotional baggage. God already knows what you've been stuffing. He's brought you to this place to heal and restore you.

As I worked through a Bible study to find healing for my sexual past, I compiled my sexual background list. I learned to take *and* give responsibility where it needed to land. There's a difference between assigning responsibility and blaming another. With the former, I'm sharing responsibility for my part and recognize that others also have responsibility in the matter. The latter blames and points the finger at another without searching one's own heart. This is unhealthy and keeps those embers burning.

Look back at your Sexual Background List. Ask God to show you who shares responsibility for the events of your sexual past – abortion, abuse, pornography, prostitution, or sexual promiscuity. (I strongly recommend dealing with your abortion wound separately. There are excellent Bible studies available. See the back of this book for recommendations.)

Whom are you angry with? Consider:
- What pain did you cause yourself?
- What did others force you to participate in?
- Who should have protected you instead of harming you?
- What were the media/cultural influences?
- Who pressured or influenced decisions you made?

In the space below, write the names of those who had a part in the events of your past. Assign responsibility where it is due. You didn't act alone. In the cases of rape or molestation, there is no responsibility to share. You were a victim of another person's sin.

This exercise may feel like you're picking open a huge scab, but it's worth the temporary pain you'll feel. God is eager to heal you. You can trust Him in this process. Begin with prayer...

 **My "I Get It!" thought for today:**

# The Smoldering Embers of Anger

## *Day 3: Housecleaning*

In yesterday's lesson, we assigned responsibility to others for the part they played in our sexual past. As a result, you may feel relieved, like a big burden has been lifted from your weary shoulders. Perhaps you feel a twinge of guilt as you struggle with the anger you feel and maintaining a Good Girl image.

As we continue on our journey of healing, it can feel much like walking or biking uphill. We start out rather energetic and before long, we are feeling out of breath and out of shape! But we are working valuable muscles and getting them into shape. You know the saying: **No Pain. No Gain.** Believe me, you have **much** to gain from Him who loves you unconditionally.

Keep pressing in hard to God. Don't give up. He will never give up on you!

> *Lord of All, I need Your strength today to keep pressing on when I want to give up. I will trust You in this process. Work miracles in my heart today. In Jesus' Name. Amen.*

Today we will begin to acknowledge and express our anger to every person in our circle. Yes, *every* person. This activity is between you and God. You will NOT read or give your letters to those you included in your circle of responsibility. There may come a time when God leads you to do so, but that time is **not now**. There have been a few women over the years that chose not to follow these instructions. The results are always disastrous as expectations are dashed, fueling more hurt and rejection. The purpose of this exercise is not to make that person know how we feel and accept responsibility for his/her actions. The purpose is to pour out your pain to God on the page before you—cutting off its power to fester and destroy you any longer.

**Guidelines for writing your letters:**
1. *Pray before writing each letter.* You want to have a sense of release from God before moving on to the next letter.
2. *Don't hurry.* There are no shortcuts around this mountain. You don't want to backtrack in your healing process. Allow yourself a few days to complete this assignment, but do start **today**!
3. *Your letter should be as long as it needs to be.* Keep writing until you've said what you need to say. He knows the depth of your anger and knows when it's been purged.
4. *Don't worry about mincing your words.* Anger is ugly. It's okay to let your language reflect the depth of your anger. Remember, we are *not* sharing with that person. If we were, our approach would be much different.
5. *Don't make excuses for bad behavior.* When writing your letters, don't make excuses for someone's bad behavior. For example: *"I hated it when you came home drunk...but I understand why you did it...your mom left the family when you were young, etc."*
   Stick to the behavior/actions that brought your pain/wound. For example: *"You took advantage of me when.... It made me feel like....."*
6. *Keep your letters in a safe place where they will not be discovered.* Some women find it difficult to go deep with their letters because they fear being discovered. If you're concerned about someone finding your letters, consider setting up a password protected lock on your computer, or secure them under your bed, in the trunk of your car, etc.

It's time to clean house. *Your* house. Or rather, your *temple*. Purge the anger. I know it can be a scary thing to go to that place. You may fear reaching the point of no return. You need to go there so you can fully grieve your losses.

The innocence lost.
    The hopes that were dashed.
        The trust that was shattered.
           The dreams that were damaged.
               The self-image that was destroyed.

Acknowledging your angry feelings may bring a sense of relief. Be on guard that we don't allow our anger to keep us in bitterness or to justify ungodly actions. God hasn't brought you to this leg of your journey to allow you to stay here. It's a layover. It's not your final destination.

> *"Come to Me, all you who are weary and burdened, and I will give you rest.*
> *Take My yoke upon you and learn from Me, for I am gentle and humble in heart, and*
> *you will find rest for your souls."*
> Matthew 11:28-29

 **My "I Get It!" thought for today:**

# The Smoldering Embers of Anger

*Day 4: Anger's Classroom*

How are you feeling after writing some anger letters to those in your circle? A bit relieved? Agitated? You may feel some relief just unloading a burden that you may not have realized was weighing you down. It's healthy to deal with our anger in the right ways. Stuffed anger, as we've learned, shows up *somewhere*, whether we're aware of it or not. It shows up in our bitter attitudes, in our bodies as depression, etc.

Today, we'll search the Scriptures to see what made God and Jesus angry and how they used their anger as a classroom to teach and not to tear down.

## God's Anger: Demonstrated

**Read the following verses and underline the words that describe or illustrate His anger.**

**Deuteronomy 29:28**—*In furious anger and in great wrath the LORD uprooted them from their land and thrust them into another land, as it is now.*

**Job 4:9**—*At the breath of God they perish; at the blast of His anger they are no more.*

**Job 9:5**—*He moves mountains without their knowing it and overturns them in His anger.*

**Psalm 78:49**—*He unleashed against them His hot anger, His wrath, indignation and hostility— a band of destroying angels.*

**Psalm 90:7**—*We are consumed by Your anger and terrified by Your indignation.*

**Using your own words, describe God's anger.**




## God's Anger: The Source
**Look up the following verses and note the reason for God's anger:**

**Deuteronomy 32:15b-17**




**Joshua 7:1-12**




**2 Chronicles 33:5-7**

**Isaiah 57:17**




**Jeremiah 25:6-7**




**Does God have cause to be angry with you? For what?**




God is love (1 John 4:8). His anger is always motivated out of love for His people. *Always.* Go back and re-read Jeremiah 25:7. The New International Version (NIV) says, *...and you have brought harm to yourself.* God punishes sin because it violates His holiness and it hurts us and others. His discipline for sin is always intended to turn our hearts back to Him.

## God's Anger: expressed
**Now let's look at how God expresses His anger. Underline key words or phrases:**

**Psalm 30: 5** – *For His anger lasts only a moment, but His favor lasts a lifetime....*

**Psalm 78:38-39** – *Yet He was merciful; He forgave their iniquities and did not destroy them. Time after time He restrained His anger and did not stir up His full wrath. He remembered that they were but flesh, a passing breeze that does not return.*

**Psalm 103:8-10** – *The Lord is compassionate and gracious, slow to anger, abounding in love. He will not always accuse, nor will He harbor his anger forever; He does not treat us as our sins deserve or repay us according to our iniquities.*

**Romans 5:6-9** – *You see, at just the right time, when we were still powerless, Christ died for the ungodly. Very rarely will anyone die for a righteous person, though for a good person someone might possibly dare to die. But God demonstrates His own love for us in this: While we were still sinners, Christ died for us. Since we have now been justified by His blood, how much more shall we be saved from God's wrath through him!*

**Are you merciful toward others who offend you or do you seek revenge? Are you quick or slow to anger? Do you harbor anger and bitterness or forgive easily?**




Examining these powerful truths causes us to see that we are all deserving of God's wrath. His power lies not only in His great ability to destroy, but also to restrain the full vent of His anger against us. It makes me want to drop to the ground and lay prostrate before the Lord in humility and gratefulness to Christ who rescues me from the coming wrath. (1 Thess. 1:10).

Let's turn now and look at Jesus. We often focus on the meek and mild side of Jesus. Did he ever get angry? And if so, what provoked his anger?

## Jesus' Anger: Demonstrated
**Read John 2:13-22 and Matthew 21:12-13 and note what made Jesus angry in the space below.**

I appreciate the Scriptures giving us this picture of Jesus. He wasn't always nicey-nicey as we tend to think. I imagine him red-faced, brows knit together, and hair whipping about as he overturned those tables—his loud, authoritative voice commanding attention. It was zeal like they'd never seen before.

Thousands of pilgrims from all over the world came to Jerusalem for Passover. In order to purchase animals for the sacrifice, these pilgrims had to exchange the currency of their home towns for the more acceptable Tyrian shekel that contained a higher percentage of silver. While exchanging the "unacceptable" coins for the Tyrian shekel, the moneychangers extracted a profit, sometimes much more than the law allowed. In addition, the merchants would set up their booths in the court of the Gentiles, making it almost impossible for them to worship God.

Jesus was angry because people were being taken advantage of. They had come to worship and were being preyed upon, robbed by greed, and squeezed out. Jesus called their shrewd business practices what it was—robbery.

## Jesus' Anger: The Source
Jesus, God-Man, felt the emotion of anger. From the Scriptures we've explored, we know that injustice was the key to His anger. He felt righteous indignation for the weak, the oppressed, the widow, and the foreigner. He cared about those who were mistreated and abused. He was for the outcast and the underdog.

**Read each of the passages below. Who was Jesus angry with and why?**

**Mark 3:1-6 NIV**

**Mark 10:13-16 NIV**

**Luke 11:37-53 NIV**

**John 11:33 NLT**

### Jesus' Anger: Expressed

Let's go back to the story of Jesus overturning the tables of the moneychangers. This time, we'll read it from the Gospel of Mark.

**Read Mark 11:15-18 NIV.**

I want you to catch one word in verse 17: **taught**. With tables and chairs flying across the marble court, coins spilling to the ground, lambs bleating, and people grumbling—Jesus *taught*. He used His anger as a classroom to instruct those with eyes to see and ears to hear.

**What do you think Jesus wanted to accomplish through this teachable moment?**

**How has (or IS) God using the consequences of your sexual past to teach you His ways?**

 My "I Get It!" thought for today:

## The Smoldering Embers of Anger

*Day 5: Battle Scars and Desires that War Within*

Today, we're going to examine what motivates our angry responses. So get your Bible and get comfortable as we close up this chapter. But first, a personal story.

One afternoon I stopped at a gas station to buy an iced coffee. As I was scouring each of the coolers for a caramel latte, I overheard a man hitting on one of the young female employees. His "come-on" was so vulgar and rude that I reacted verbally with a loud *"ugh!"* I felt instant disgust and anger. I was *livid*! I whipped around to see a man who appeared to be about 70 years of age directing his comments to a woman who was young enough to be his granddaughter. She looked barely 21.

As I made my way to the checkout line, he was right in front of me. I glared at the back of his head, judging him harshly. He was totally oblivious to the impact of his words or to my anger. I tried to sort through my racing thoughts to come up with something that would put him in his place. He paid for his beer and left. I said nothing to him, although I talked with the young lady about the incident.

On my drive home, I cried as I told God how I felt. I was angry and disgusted at that "dirty old man." I was angry at myself for not confronting him. I was angry at not showing courage when it counted most. I was angry at missing an opportunity to stand up for this young woman and model the power of using one's voice.

Pondering this incident days later, I wondered with God, *"What are you trying to teach me? What do you want to show me? This isn't the first time I've heard or seen things like that. What makes this time so different?"*

As I rehearsed that incident at the gas station over and over, instead of staying in disgust-mode, I began praying for that man to know God's love and forgiveness. I thought about his actions and what could be underneath it all. What I believe God was showing me is that this man, in all his years, is still looking for what every heart longs for—**LOVE.**

Wasn't that my *own* desire? My search may have looked different from his, but my craving heart had led me to look for love in all the wrong places—to all the wrong people. I had looked for someone—*anyone*—to satisfy a longing that only God could ultimately satisfy. If I peeled away the distasteful language and coarse approach, is that man really so different from me? Is he really so different from you?

So this is where we'll camp out today. We'll look inside our hearts and see what motivates our angry responses—to what wars within us.

> **Let's pray:** *Lord, peel away the scabs and callouses—those hard places of my heart—so that I can see what You see. Show me Your ways, Lord, teach me Your paths. Fill my desires with You. In Jesus' Name. Amen.*

Our angry responses appear justified when something happens *to* us. Let's face it; we're not provoked to anger when things go our way. Rather, we get angry when we don't get what we *want*.

Let's look at Scripture to see what *does* trigger our angry responses and how to overcome them.

**Write out James 4:1-3 NIV**

**According to verse 1, what wars (or battles) within us?**

**Looking back at the circle in which you assigned responsibility, what desires were unmet by those within your circle? What did you <u>want</u> that you didn't get?**

**In what ways did you quarrel, fight, nag, or manipulate for those desires to be met?**

True and not-so-proud story:
Long before I became a Christ-follower, I was dating a man whom I thought I wanted to marry. We had been dating for two years, and I thought it was time he get his act together and make a commitment to me. I did many things to prove myself worthy of matrimony. I cleaned his house, cooked him dinner, etc. Still no commitment.

Feeling hurt and angry that my desires were not being met, I did something pathetic: I sent myself flowers. The card simply said: **From a Secret Admirer.**

When he called me at work, I "graciously" thanked him for the beautiful bouquet. The conversation went just as I'd imagined it would. He'd say he didn't send them. I'd pretend to be surprised and wonder aloud, *"Hmmm. Who could be my 'Secret Admirer'?"*

Don't judge me.
    I told you it was pathetic.

The conversation did go just as I'd imagined, but the outcome totally failed. My manipulative actions didn't produce the results I'd wanted. I wanted him to be jealous and spur him on to decision-making action. Neither happened.

Thankfully, God protected me from what would have surely been a failed marriage. But that true and not-so-proud story revealed a legitimate desire that battled within me: love, acceptance, and commitment through marriage.

I had elevated men to God-like status. (For the record, you should know that what you elevate highly governs you. God calls it idolatry.) I sought their attention, acceptance, affection, and love—much to my detriment. When men failed to give me what I wanted, it felt like rejection and abandonment. Those negative feelings gave way to quarreling, fighting, bitterness, criticism, and even hatred.

**Have you elevated a human relationship above a relationship with God? Who have you pursued more than God? What did (or do) you want more than God?**

Our anger not only rises from our circumstances (like sins committed against you), but also from the desires at war within us. We feel angry when we don't get what we want, because ultimately, our motives are selfish. We control and manipulate to get what we want. When we don't get what we want, look out! All hell breaks loose—around us and within us.

In my two-year relationship, I was hurt and angry because I didn't get what I wanted: commitment and love. His lack of commitment to me fueled the lies I believed about myself—that I was flawed and unlovable.

**What lies did you believe as a result of your unfulfilled desires?**




Looking back to the story of the old man at the gas station, it took some peeling away to get to the bottom of why I was so angry. On the surface, defending the dignity of a young woman looked and felt like "righteous anger."

But after peeling it down another layer or two, it triggered a deeply rooted lie in my heart that I believed about men in general: that all men are selfish and just looking to score.

Sweet friend, God is *always* speaking to us. Let us have ears to hear and eyes to see. Your anger is shouting to your soul that you are hurt, that something's not right. Your anger can be the classroom by which He teaches you if you will allow Him access into that dark closet.

Slow down and process your anger with Him. Not just the big stuff, but the little frustrations and the negative self-talk. They are indicators that something's not right. They are signals of the soul. God wants to process those things with you. He wants you to know the truth so it can set you free. (John 8:32) Isn't it time to stop covering it up? Isn't it time to stop doing the same things and expecting different results?

Maybe you're nodding in agreement but not at all sure how to do this. Here's what God showed me as I repeatedly cried out to Him about my anger:

**Start an anger journal**. Use it only for this purpose. God gifted me with a new journal from my best friend. It had a beautiful cover and one word on it: **BREATHE...** It couldn't have been more perfect. It's exactly what I needed to *do*.

Through prayer, God showed me what was important to process. The three points all begin with E.R. When in crisis, where do we go? The E.R.! And **He** is our Great Physician.

1. **Event & Response**: Record the incident that made you angry. How did you respond or react to the event? Did you have an outburst? Or did you stuff it? What did you say to yourself through negative self-talk?
2. **Examine Responses**: Ask yourself why the incident made you angry. How did it make you feel? (Loss of control, fear, offended, etc.) Keep asking yourself why. When you identify the feeling, again ask yourself why... (Ex. Underneath anger may be fear.)
3. **Excavate Roots**: Process the entire incident with God. Ask Him what He wants you to see through the event. What lies have you believed?
   Recognize it.
       Repent of it.
       Replace it with God's truth.

I'm praying that you will be set free from the destructive tangle-hold of anger and negative self-talk from believing Satan's lies. We all have our battle scars, but remember that Christ bore on His body the ultimate scars that have set you free from sin and death!

**My "I Get It!" thought for today:**

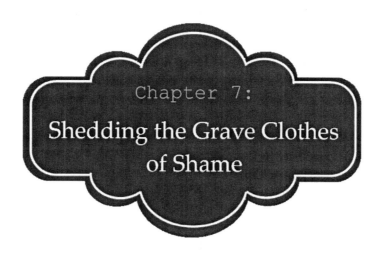

Chapter 7:
Shedding the Grave Clothes of Shame

# Shedding the Grave Clothes of Shame

---∞---

*Day 1: Exposing Shame*

Shame. For some, just saying this word aloud can conjure up unpleasant feelings. Shame is the deeply held belief that one's being is flawed. Biblically, shame means to dishonor or disgrace. It can manifest itself as a feeling of not being good enough no matter how hard we try, of not feeling worthy, and of not being lovable. Shame can also be well-disguised.[1] Even people who appear to have it all together can be bound with shame.

If we have grown up with deep feelings of shame, we will recognize its impact and the many ways it has disrupted our lives. Shame attacks in three primary areas:[2]
1. Our identity (our sense of who we are)
2. Our intimacy with others
3. Our self-esteem

**In the following chart, circle the indicators of shame that you recognize in yourself.**

## Common Indicators of Shame[3]

| |
|---|
| Feeling exposed |
| Feeling like a fraud |
| Having no voice |
| Feeling powerless |
| Having to cover up |
| Feeling foolish |
| Wanting to disappear or be invisible |
| Feeling too needy |
| Feeling too vulnerable |
| Difficulty accepting praise (*"If you really knew what I was like..."*) |
| Taking criticism very hard |
| Being a people-pleaser (*feeling very tired, very busy, yet very reluctant to say "no"*) |
| Rarely giving honest feedback for fear of hurting others |
| Inability to defend oneself against injustice |
| Inability to defend oneself against misunderstanding in the face of authority |
| Putting oneself down in conversations |
| Procrastinating out of fear of criticism or because *"I won't get it right..."* |
| **Vulnerable to depression** because so many feelings are buried to avoid the reprimand, punishment, rejection or isolation that will occur if they are honest |
| Possibly struggling with addictions and compulsive behaviors |
| Avoiding true intimacy with others because it may reveal how defective and flawed we really are |
| Placing high expectations on others to know what they need |
| Inability to ask for what they want |
| Having "needs" is considered shameful |
| Having a very high or very low expectation of self and/or others |
| Persistent feeling of being "on guard" or "watched" |
| Relaxing or self-care is difficult or impossible |

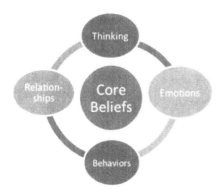

The diagram to the left shows how shame can affect our thinking, emotions, behaviors, and ultimately, our relationships. But at the root of it all, shame attacks our core beliefs. Our beliefs are the foundation on which our ways of thinking are shaped. **Read 2 Corinthians 10:4-5 from The Message. Identify and underline any of the Belief Building Blocks.**

*The world is unprincipled. It's dog-eat-dog out there! The world doesn't fight fair. But we don't live or fight our battles that way—never have and never will. The tools of our trade aren't for marketing or manipulation, but they are for demolishing that entire massively corrupt culture. We use our powerful God-tools for smashing warped philosophies, tearing down barriers erected against the truth of God, fitting every loose thought and emotion and impulse into the structure of life shaped by Christ. Our tools are ready at hand for clearing the ground of every obstruction and building lives of obedience into maturity.*

**What are you learning about the relationship between our thoughts, emotions, and behavior?**

**Read 2 Corinthians 10:4-5 from a different version. What are we to do with our thoughts?**

In the Daily Hope devotional **Practice the Principle of Replacement,**[4] Rick Warren says,

> Our minds are really an amazing creation. It would take a computer the size of a small city just to carry out the basic functions of our brain.
>
> You're also constantly talking to yourself. Research indicates that most people speak at a rate of 150 to 200 words per minute, but the mind can process about 500 to 600 words a minute.
>
> The problem is that a lot of us are like Job, who says, "Everything I say seems to condemn me" (Job 9:20 GN). He's saying, in effect, "Everything I say puts me down." If you are a typical human being, you are your own worst critic. We're always putting ourselves down. We walk into a room smiling, but inside we're thinking, "I'm fat. I'm dumb. I'm ugly. And I'm always late!"

Shame is one of those things that 2 Corinthian 10:4-5 speaks of as an argument that must be demolished. The KJV uses the phrase: "casting down imaginations." An imagination is an image in your mind that is incorrect. For example, if you are talking about yourself negatively, as we just read in the excerpt above, you've got an imagination that needs to be cast down.

The Hebrew meaning of the word **imagination** is *a reckoning; reasoning; a judgment.* To cast down means *to pull down, demolish the subtle reasoning (of opponents) likened to a fortress.*

**How has shame and negative thinking been a fortress in your mind?**

**According to 2 Corinthians 10:4, what kind of weapons do we have access to?**

**Pray and ask God to reveal the following and record your insights below:**

- Warped philosophies
- Barriers that have been erected against God's Word
- Obstacles to accepting the truth of His Word, the truth of who you are and the truth of who He is.

**Conclude by writing out John 8:32.**

Start believing what God says about you. When you find a verse in the Bible that speaks to you, write it down on a card or in your journal. Memorize that truth and pray it back to God: "Father, thank you that I am fearfully and wonderfully made and worth redeeming."

 **My "I Get It!" thought for today:**

## Shedding the Grave Clothes of Shame

### *Day 2: Identity Theft*

Identity theft is a growing crime around the world. About 8 million Americans are victimized each year – that's roughly 1 person every 3 seconds. Identity theft is not just about stealing someone's money or assets – it's about stealing her name and reputation. It's the fastest-growing crime and costs Americans over $50 billion in fraudulent charges every year. Scores of businesses, banks, and consumers take special precautions (and spend plenty of money) to avoid becoming victims.

Scanning the web on this topic led me to numerous sites that promised help for *Identity Theft Protection* and *Identity Theft Solutions*. But the one I was most drawn to says:

> ***Identity Theft Recovery***
> *Get your identity back now. Stop being a victim.*

You can probably guess where we're going with this subject. But before we go any further, let's ask our Heavenly Father to open our eyes:

> *Lord of all Creation, You are glorious! Open up my eyes to see who I really am in You. Open my ears and my heart to recognize Truth. Help me to reject the lies I've believed and embrace my **true** identity. In Jesus' Name. Amen.*

Have you ever been a victim of identity theft? Hopefully not. However, many of us *live* as victims of identity theft. We have believed lies that others have said through their actions or words toward us. And we've also believed our own negative self-talk. We have denied our true identity as one made in the image of God.

In yesterday's lesson, you discovered areas in which shame may be rearing its ugly head in your life. Shame is not our true identity. It is a learned belief about self. Shame is an unholy perspective of who we really are in God. It is an obstacle to intimacy with Him because shame keeps us barricaded behind walls of self-protection.

Shame enters the scene as a result of the ways we've processed the pain of our past. And our past is not our past if it is still a part of our present. We need a new identity. Not one created by the world, but one based on our original intent and design; an identity based on Whose we are.

---

**Merriam Webster Dictionary**
**Identity**: *the state of being exactly alike; sameness*
Synonyms include: individuality, character, uniqueness, distinctiveness

---

To have our identity renewed, we cannot deny our story – the how-I-got-here parts of our story. In the book **Rid of My Disgrace**, authors Justin and Lindsey Holcomb state, *"Story is powerful. The link between story and identity cannot be overstated. If the trauma of your story becomes **the** story about you, then your identity will be founded on disgrace."*[5]

Our identity must not be defined by past wounds. Nor is it meant to be shaped by self-love, self-reliance, or self-help to overcome your negative story.

There is another story.

The Holcombs continue, *"To experience healing and freedom, your identity must be established on the work of Christ, not on the foundation of the shame and self-hate that frequently results from (our story). You need to know God's statements and images about who you are, not self-produced positive statements or the lies being told to you by your experience of disgrace."*[6]

God offers the redemptive story told in Scripture. The identity from that story is founded on grace in at least three specific ways:[7]

1. **Image of God.** As the crown of God's creation, humans reveal God more beautifully than any other creatures. We have inherent dignity and self-worth because we are made in the image *of* God.

   **Write out the following Scriptures and commit them to heart and to memory:**

   Genesis 1:26-27

   Psalm 139:14

Psalm 139 may be very familiar to you. Don't rush past it. The word *fearfully* in the Hebrew text means *astonishment and awe, to inspire reverence or Godly fear.* Instead of seeing your flaws, a good look at oneself should inspire us to worship God for His amazing handiwork. Consider how your organs function, your brain reasons, etc. *Wow!*

2. **People of God/Children of God.** God calls us many things that convey value and acceptance, but perhaps the most intimate is to be called a child of God.

   Psalm 95:7-8

   Ezekiel 37:23

   Zechariah 2:8

   Romans 8:15-16

   1 Peter 2:9-10

3. **Righteousness of God.** God uses dramatic words to describe those who are His. Underline your discoveries.

   Isaiah 43:1

   2 Corinthians 5:17

   Ephesians 2:10

   Ephesians 5:27

   1 Thessalonians 5:5

   2 Corinthians 5:21

   Colossians 1:21-22

Our identity *in Christ* is deeper than any of our wounds. Hallelujah! That is good news!

We need Someone to rescue us from our sin and self-reliance and restore to us the identity that has been lost. You have an amazing God-story to tell. Go tell it!

*Let the redeemed of the LORD tell their story – those He redeemed from the hand of the foe...* Psalm 107:2

 **My "I Get It!" thought for today:**

## Shedding the Grave Clothes of Shame

### *Day 3: Water & Whine*

In this week's lesson, we have defined shame and exposed how it can manifest itself in our lives. If you've been wrapped up in shame, you need to recover your lost identity. It's time for an intervention.

> **Merriam Webster Dictionary**
> **Intervention:** *to come in between; to interfere with the outcome or course especially of a condition or process (as to prevent harm or improve functioning)*
> Synonyms include: involvement, intercession

**Let's seek His face:** *Lord, if ever I needed Your intervention – it is now. My emotions can be a jumbled mess at times, leading me to believe that I'm worse or better than I really am. Help me to see things in my life that have blocked my relationship with You, rather than bringing me closer. In Jesus' Name. Amen.*

In today's lesson, we'll peer over Jesus' shoulder and more than likely find a familiar face looking back. Open your Bible and read John 4:4-30, 39-42. The story is no doubt a familiar one. The woman at the well could be your story. My story.

Let's walk through these passages together. And as we do, I encourage you to read it a few times.
- First, read it as an observer – watching Jesus interact with this Samaritan woman.
- Read it a second time, putting yourself in the woman's place – engaging your emotions. What might it have been like to wear her dusty sandals for a day?
- Third, read it through Jesus' eyes. What did He see in the woman? What did He want to do in her life? In *your* life?

The following narrative will be a mix of biblical history, and my own imagination. Perhaps God will use this combination to point out something He so lovingly wants us to see.

### Read John 4:4-6

To go from Judea to Galilee meant passing through Samaria. Most Jews did everything they could to avoid travelling through Samaria. The reason dated many years earlier when the northern kingdom, with its capital at Samaria, fell to the Assyrians. Many Jews were exiled to Assyria, and foreigners were brought in to settle the land to help keep the peace (2 Kings 17:24). What resulted from those foreigners and the remaining Jews was a mixed race, impure in the opinion of Jews who lived in the southern kingdom. The Samaritans had even created their own place of worship on Mount Gerizim to parallel the temple at Jerusalem.

Even though there was long-standing prejudice between Jews and Samaritans, Jesus didn't allow it to color his views. On the contrary, His Life was for *all* people, *all* nations – Jew and Gentile alike.

Why do you think Jesus went through Samaria? Because it was a shortcut? It *was* a shorter route. If distance was the issue, His encounter with the Samaritan woman could be earmarked as a *coincidence* – purely happenstance. Or maybe Jesus was on a mission? If so, Jesus' meeting with the woman at the well would have been *intentional*. And if it was intentional, there was something He planned to do for her.

*Intervention Question*

**The book you are holding in your hands right now: Is it happenstance? Or do you think God divinely orchestrated an intentional act of grace in your life? Write out your thoughts.**

### Read John 4:7-8

Women of her day came to draw water early in the morning when it was cool. It was probably a social time for the women as well. But this woman came at the hottest time of day to draw water. Imagine her walking across the village with her head held high. Not because she thought she was better than others, but rather because she was determined not to allow anyone the gratification of getting to her. Over the years, she grew to have a tough exterior. Growing up, perhaps she felt invisible. Now she wished she really was. But it was not so. Her reputation was public knowledge. Her skeletons in the closet were in plain view for all to see. She kept walking, eyes looking straight ahead, her face expressionless.

She probably knew no one would be at the well that time of day. She would be safe from the sneers and whispers, safe from the derogatory comments. At least for a short while. She was rejected among a rejected people. It didn't get much lonelier than that.

As she busied herself with her work, maybe she got lost in her thoughts. That is, until she heard a man's voice. Did she blink back her surprise as she realized a *Jewish man* was speaking to her? Not many people spoke to her – and certainly not Jews.

*Intervention Question*

**How has your sexual past contributed to having a tough exterior (in appearance, dress, attitude, etc.)? Whom have you avoided for fear of judgment?**

### Read John 4:9-12

God's gift of grace is for the outcast, the shunned, and the scorned. Sadly, the Samaritan woman didn't see Jesus as He was – the Fountain of Living Water. She only saw a poor, weary traveler. And a *Jew* at that.

Her exchange with Jesus sounds to me a little irritated. A little sarcastic. A little angry, albeit controlled. Reading between the lines, I hear what she may have thought: *Who do you think you are? You're just another big-shot Jew who thinks he knows it all. You don't even have a cup to draw water with, let alone a bucket. What makes you think I believe you can give me "living" water? You're just another man making promises you won't make good on.*

*Intervention Question*

**In what ways have you rejected God's truth about your sexual past because you didn't like how it was "packaged" (the person, the delivery, the message, the conviction you felt, etc.)?**

**Read John 4:13-15**

Several Old Testament Scriptures speak of thirsting after God as one thirsts for water. Jesus was claiming to be the Messiah. Only the Messiah could give the gift that satisfies the soul's desire.

But the woman totally missed what Jesus was offering her. If we're honest, we have done the same thing a million times over. We miss our *true* needs for our felt needs. True needs reflect the soul like a lake reflects the sky above. The Samaritan woman jumped on His offer but for all the wrong reasons. She may have wanted an escape from the routine of drawing water every day...relief from having to walk across the village enduring the whispers, stares, and sneers of others. I wonder if deep down she thought, *"Oh please give me this water! Fix this mess I'm in so I won't have to keep coming here to draw water!"*

Jesus knew her true need was to have a genuine God-relationship that would satisfy her need for love, security and belonging. It was the answer to her search for significance, her search for love in all the wrong places. And He knows it's your true need, too. Our loving heavenly Father wants us to see the *root* of our desperate needs. Otherwise, we will keep coming to a well that won't satisfy the real cravings of our soul. When the cravings of our soul aren't met in Christ, we go looking for satisfaction in lots of different places – empty places. And those empty places cause more craving.

*Intervention Question*

**Where has your need for love, acceptance, and belonging led you? What is your soul craving?**

 My "I Get It!" thought for today:

## Shedding the Grave Clothes of Shame

### Day 4: An Abandoned Water Jar

Today we're going to pick up where we left off in the story of the woman at the well. It's a story of an unexpected intervention.

**Let's pray:** *Lord, I'm thirsty. Open my eyes and my heart to respond to Your words of life. I want to drink deeply. In Jesus' Name. Amen.*

### Read John 4:16-20

How would you feel if suddenly someone knew something about you that was no longer hidden? A little exposed? Vulnerable? The Samaritan woman did what I would do: she swallowed hard, blinked back her surprise, and changed the subject.

Anyone else may have relented to her diversion tactic, but not Jesus. Remember, "*...He needed to go through Samaria*" (vs. 4 NKJV). And she desperately needed an intervention, although she didn't know it. How interesting that the person who needs an intervention is the last one to realize it. But Jesus knew it. He came to show Himself as the Messiah for all people – the Jews, the Samaritans, the outcasts, the broken, the used, and the users.

Jesus' request to bring back her husband was not meant to shame her. That wasn't His way. It was aimed at exposing her real need – the craving of her soul. In the words of Bible Scholar Matthew Henry, "*(Jesus) sets himself to awaken her conscience, to open the wound of guilt; so that she would more easily apprehend the remedy by grace.*"

In Jesus' day, husbands had the role of teaching spiritual truths to their wives so that they may know and understand. The fact that she had no husband was the point that Jesus wanted to draw out in order to bring conviction of sin and the forgiveness that follows.

### Intervention Question

**Have you been unmoved by God's Truth in the area of your sexual past or in your current relationship(s)?**

### Read John 4:21-26

With her lifestyle exposed, the woman brings up a popular theological issue between the Jews and Samaritans. But it was another smokescreen to her deepest need, her soul craving. She was stuck on knowing the *right place* to worship. We still have those kinds of arguments today between various denominations within Christianity. What's the right denomination? What's the right style of worship? We have this need to have all the right answers.

But Jesus pares it all down to having a right heart attitude. True worship is about *how* we worship. "*You desire truth in the inward parts*" (Psalm 51:6 NKJV) is our invitation to stop lying to ourselves that we're better or worse than we think we are. Come, let's admit our real needs, our imperfections and the lies that we've believed about ourselves, others, sex, relationships, and God so that we can worship Him in **truth**.

*Intervention Questions*

**In what ways am I claiming God is my Sufficiency while still looking to satisfy my needs in my own way?**

**In what ways do I say that I trust God yet obsess over my circumstances or past wounds?**

**Am I selective in the Scriptures I believe? Do I embrace the promises of God and reject those that make me uncomfortable or demand action?**

**Is there evidence in my life to support that unresolved hurt has hardened my heart?**

In spite of her overt diversion tactics, the woman at the well admitted to wanting more than just answers. She confessed to looking for the Messiah who *"...is coming...and will explain everything to us"* (vs 25). Jesus did not keep His identity hidden from her. He boldly declared, "I...AM he."

Are you looking for the I AM in *your* story?

**Read John 4:28-29, 39-42**

She left her water jar and went back to town to tell others. She came that day for water as she had done daily. But that hot afternoon was different. An unexpected intervention led to her:

Secrets exposed.

Thirst quenched.

    Feet on a new path.

        Life-changing testimony.

*Intervention Question*

**The Samaritan woman came to draw water yet in the end left her water jar behind. What is the Lord asking you to leave behind?**

This week, we've been talking about shame. What does this story have to do with shame? There's no mention of shame in the story. The woman never asks Jesus to remove her shame, nor does Jesus say, "Woman, your shame is gone. Go in peace." So why have we looked at this story in our discussion of shame?

Shame often results from sin. Our levels of shame can teeter-totter if we base our worth on how well things are going in the relationship. If it's going well, we're feeling good about ourselves. If the relationship is struggling, our perception of self is fragile too. And that can be the very thing that drives us from relationship to relationship only to repeat the cycle again. We begin to judge our worth and wonder, "What's wrong with me?" However, measuring our worth by any other means than being made in the image of Christ and who we are in Him will make us people-pleasers rather than God-pleasers.

How do you think the Samaritan woman felt about herself after five failed relationships? Add to that the sneers, jeers, and rejection from other people and she probably felt her worth sink to new depths. Like the Samaritan woman, we can wear shame and rejection like an ugly, worn out coat.

As the Spirit of God brings conviction to our hearts, draw near to Him. Come clean and be clean. It's time to recover our true identity in Christ.

As I was working through my own restorative process, I clearly remember thinking: *I know I'm forgiven by God. But I guess the shame I still feel is a consequence of my sin, and I'm just going to have to accept it.*

Wrong.

The enemy wanted very much for me to think there was no remedy for my shame.

And then I came across a verse that changed it all for me:

*Do not be deceived: Neither the sexually immoral nor idolaters nor adulterers nor men who have sex with men, nor thieves nor the greedy nor drunkards nor slanderers nor swindlers will inherit the kingdom of God. And that is what some of you were. But you were washed, you were sanctified, you were justified in the name of the Lord Jesus Christ and by the Spirit of our God* (I Corinthians 6:9-11).

There was one vital key that I had overlooked in my reasoning: *I belonged to Christ*. Certainly I saw myself in that list. The good news in the midst of the muck seemed to leap off the page as I read it: "*...and that is what some of you were.*" You might want to read it again and underline it for yourself. If you see yourself in that list of sin, you may be tempted to feel depressed. But if you are in Christ, that is what you *were*. "**But you were washed, you were sanctified, you were justified in the name of the Lord Jesus Christ and by the Spirit of our God!**"

We'll close with one final Scripture. **Read Isaiah 54:1-8 and list the promises of God.**

Are you ready to exchange those filthy rags of shame for the robe that is yours because of Christ? Go ahead and put it on.

You.

    Look.

        Beautiful.

 **My "I Get It!" thought for today:**

## Shedding the Grave Clothes of Shame

### Day 5 – *The Great Liberation*

*The thief comes only to steal and kill and destroy; I have come that they may have life, and have it to the full.*
John 10:10

---
**Merriam Webster Dictionary**
**Sabotage:** *the act of destroying or damaging something deliberately so that it does not work correctly*
Synonyms: damage, disrupt, interrupt, impair

---

From the beginning, Satan has been actively working out schemes of theft, murder and destruction against God's children (John 10:10). Through our own sinful choices and those committed against us, Satan delights in our wounds, pain and captivity. He sabotages marriages, families, and the innocence of children and adolescents. He strips.

 He exploits.

  He accuses.

   He demoralizes.

Satan intends our harm. He's bent on damaging our identity and dignity—deterring our deliverance. Satan hopes our responses to hurt will cause us to cower, run, and hide. Let us do *anything* but run to Christ. For when we turn to Him, we will discover the truth about our worth. And we'll find hope.

Yet despite man's rebellion against God, He had a plan to redeem fallen man to bring him close once again. His plan was methodical, intentional, and deliberate. It was executed with precision. God's plan would ultimately sabotage Satan's cruel grip of hatred toward mankind and break his suffocating yoke forever.

God's plan was crucifixion: A spotless Lamb offered for the sins of all people, for all time. *The reason the Son of God appeared was to destroy the devil's work* (1 John 3:8b)...*and having disarmed the powers and authorities, He made a public spectacle of them, triumphing over them by the cross* (Colossians 2:15). But God didn't stop with the crucifixion. The **resurrection** was His holy trump card. Through it, we are made new and have the glorious promise of eternity.

Through Christ's redemption...

 He forgives our sins.

  He restores our dignity.

   He gives peace and hope.

    He clothes us in His righteousness.

     He adopts us as His own for all eternity.

*What good news this is to my soul, Father. Let the power of its truth resound in my heart. Open my eyes to see that the prison doors have been unlocked, and I am free. Help me to know the love of the One who rescues me and the resolve to truly live as one set free. In Jesus' Name. Amen.*

Considering the gory crucifixion of Christ on the cross arouses within me a deeper understanding of His love. At times I have asked in my heart, *"Lord, **why** would you do this? Are we worth all this?"*

What about you? Have you wondered the same things? Are you struggling to believe He would die for your sins, including your sexual past?

**Write out the following verses:**

John 15:13

John 10:18

John 3:16

Though this may be difficult to read and certainly more gruesome than any R-rated film Hollywood could produce, I believe understanding Christ's crucifixion is an important piece to our healing journey.

Crucifixion was an ancient method of execution in which the victim's hands and feet were bound and nailed to a cross. It was one of the most horribly painful methods of capital punishment and was considered a most shameful and disgraceful way to die (Deut. 21:23).

Scourging was the prelude to crucifixion. Roman scourging's were ordinarily very severe, not limited to forty stripes as among the Jews. Whips with small pieces of metal or bone at the tips were used and could easily cause serious trauma, such as ripping pieces of flesh from the body or loss of an eye. Besides causing severe pain, the victim would approach a state of shock due to loss of blood.

**Look up the following verses. Though you may be very familiar with the crucifixion of Christ, take the time to read the verses as they are listed.**

Deuteronomy 25:3
John 19:1
Isaiah 50:6

In Jesus' case, the Roman soldiers went beyond their orders to whip Him. They also mocked His claim as King by placing a crown of thorns upon His head and a royal robe upon His shoulders.

John 19:2-3

The condemned were always stripped naked to intensify their shame. In the culture of that day, it was considered shameful for men to expose an ankle, much less their thigh. Hanging on a tree outside Jerusalem on a main road (John 19:17), thousands of people would have witnessed His nakedness, His shame.

### John 19:23-24

The nails used in crucifixion were tapered iron spikes approximately 5 to 7 inches long. It's unfathomable to think that those condemned to die could take anywhere from a few hours to a few *days* to die. The dead body was left up for vultures and other birds to consume. The Romans often broke the prisoner's legs to hasten death and usually forbade burial. However, according to Scripture, we know that Jesus' legs were not broken.

### John 19:31-34
### Isaiah 53:5

Jesus was abused in all ways – physically, verbally, and emotionally.

He was abandoned.
    He was beaten.
        He was rejected.
            He was insulted.
                He was degraded.
                    He was spat upon.
                        He was lonely and alone.
                            He was tempted in every way.

There is nothing we may feel from our past which Jesus cannot identify. Scripture tells us that Jesus endured temptation in all things but did not sin (Hebrews 2:18, 4:15). He experienced many of the same *emotions* we experience that have resulted from our sexual past (like rejection, insult, abandonment, etc.) though He never sinned sexually.

There are two more Scriptures that we will look at which I hope will put an exclamation mark at the end of our lesson.

*For the joy set before Him He endured the cross, scorning its shame,*
*and sat down at the right hand of the throne of God.*
### Hebrews 12:2b

Remarkably, Jesus was *glad* to endure the cross – that's what joy means. He bore the pain of His scourging and the humiliation of the cross bravely and calmly. And by doing so, Jesus scorned the shame. Some translations use the word *disregard* or *despise*. All of these words can mean "hate, ignore, snub, overlook, rebuke, disdain" or "to think little or nothing of." So this verse can mean: *Jesus ignored the shame. He hated the shame – He overlooked its insult.* At its core, Jesus rebuked the shame of *all* sin for *all* mankind. He looked beyond the here-and-now toward what His obedience on the cross would accomplish for us.

What does all of this mean for us?

The shame of every violent assault against you...
The shame of every violent assault committed by you...
The shame of every unplanned pregnancy...
The shame of every abortion...
The shame of discovery or exposure...

The shame of imprisonment...
The shame of every adulterous relationship...
The shame of every humiliating act forced upon you...
The shame of every degrading act performed by you...
The shame of every sexual act outside marriage...
The shame of every outburst...
The shame of self-harm...
The shame of *every* sinful act...
The shame of _____ (fill in the blank)

**Nailed to the cross.**
    **Not just the sin, but the shame too.**

Sin and shame are two distinctly different things. Shame is brought on by sin but can be the result of someone sinning against us – as in the cases of sexual assault (child abuse, rape, etc.). The price for our sin and shame has been <u>paid in full</u>. There is nothing else to be offered for it. No other payment is acceptable. You can't work for it. You can't be good enough to earn it.

Jesus has triumphed over death and sin! He conquered so that we could overcome.

*...having disarmed the powers and authorities, he made a public spectacle of them,*
*triumphing over them by the cross.*
Colossians 2:15

He finds you acceptable and pleasing. Yes, you. He has taken your sin and shame and washed it away. Jesus is the Righteous One who has recovered your lost identity. You can find it only in Him. *Those who look to Him are radiant; their faces are never covered with shame (Psalm 34:5).*

Because of Jesus, our prison doors are open. Today is the day of our great liberation!

 **My "I Get It!" thought for today:**

# Embracing Forgiveness

### Day 1: *Masterpieces of Grace*

In a previous chapter, we looked at the destructive nature of shame. My hope is that we are moving past that false identity and living in the freedom and reality of our **new** identity as a Daughter of God.

As we move into our new topic on forgiveness, shedding our old robe of shame has never been more important. Shame is like a tarp that hinders us from getting drenched by the Living Water that is meant to cleanse and wash us; to keep us from receiving Christ's forgiveness. The crucifixion of Christ was the door to our salvation, our forgiveness. The blood of Christ was shed for the remission of sins (Matthew 26:28). Daughter, if you are *in* Christ, you are **forgiven**.

But, but… "I don't *feel* forgiven." Forgiveness is not a feeling. It's a *fact*. And sweet sister, it's a **gift**. We *receive* a gift and *earn* a paycheck (Romans 4:4 NLT). Not the other way around.

> **Let's pray:** *Lord, let the truth of Christ's sacrifice change the way I see myself. My hands and my heart are wide open. Fill me. Move me. Change me. In Jesus' Name. Amen.*

As we begin, let's define forgiveness:

---
**Merriam Webster Dictionary**
**Forgive:** *to stop feeling anger toward (someone who has done something wrong); to stop blaming someone; to stop requiring payment*
Synonyms: pardon, acquit, clear

---

This is what God through Christ chose to grant you and me. He lay upon Jesus the penalty that we deserved, who paid it in full. His wrath satisfied. The guilty now pardoned.

Jesus cried out from the cross, *"It is finished!"* Jews in that day used this accounting term in the marketplace. Merchants didn't provide sales receipts to their customers. Instead, when a transaction was made, the merchant would yell loudly for all to hear: *"It is finished!"* It meant that the sale was paid in full; the buyer could not be accused of stealing. So as Jesus hung on the cross and cried out these three final words (John 19:30), He was clearly stating that His body and blood had purchased mankind. He was the sacrificial Passover Lamb. It is finished! Forgiven!

**Write out Hebrews 9:22.**

**Read Ephesians 2:4-10. According to this passage, what in God's character compels Him to be forgiving?**

**Is there any requirement on our part to receive His grace?**

**In the above passage, underline the reason(s) for His great show of grace.**

Though many of us have the head-knowledge of Ephesians 2:8, we may struggle to secure it in our hearts. Regrettably, some of us are still working to earn God's grace and forgiveness. Messages from our growing years echo in our minds:

*"There's no free lunch."*
*"Something worth getting is worth working for."*

In the right context, these are great principles to live by. But when we look at them in light of our topic at hand, we apply these principles to our own detriment.

From cover to cover, Scripture repeatedly reveals God's merciful nature that gives us what we do not deserve: forgiveness. Read and write out the following verses:

**Isaiah 38:17**

**Isaiah 43:25**

**Isaiah 44:22**

**Micah 7:18-19**

**Colossians 1:13-14**

**1 John 1:9**

**What did you learn about God and His forgiveness from these passages?**

Let's look at one final passage today. Psalm 103 is a beautiful psalm from start to finish. It shows off God's attributes and a long list of Believers' "benefits" which are better than any 401k!

**In the space below, list out the benefits or gifts that are yours as a Daughter of God.**

All of it is yours. There is no place for shame. May these truths crowd it out of every dark corner so you can soak in His great love for you.

At the beginning of today's homework, we looked at Ephesians 2:4-10. Verses 7 and 10 reveal God's purpose in lavishing upon us His grace and mercy. Take a look at those verses again. You are on display, showing off for God all that He has done in your life and will continue to do. Not feeling like a masterpiece? It's not about feelings, but fact. We are masterpieces of His grace *"showing the world the incomparable riches of his grace expressed in his kindness to us, in Christ Jesus."*

 **My "I Get It!" thought for today:**

## Embracing Forgiveness

### Day 2: Fault Lines

Put on your science hat and let's do a quick review on fault lines. Remember those? A fault line is a point where the earth's plates meet or lay against each other. The movements of the earth along these lines produce earthquakes. The World Dictionary defines a fault line as *a potentially disruptive division or area of contention.* Yikes! Those living near them are well aware of the dangers that can arise.

So why the quick study on fault lines? We'll get to that. But first...

> **Let's pray**: *Father, you alone know the fault lines and faulty thinking I have about You, sin, and forgiveness. Show me where my faith is shaky and help me to throw off anything that is holding me back from living as a forgiven Daughter of God. In Jesus' Name. Amen.*

Do you have an easier time of forgiving others or accepting God's forgiveness for yourself? Have you ever said to yourself or confessed to someone else: *"I just can't seem to forgive myself for..."*?

**What are you having a hard time forgiving yourself for? Why?**

Secular psychologists endorse the idea that we must learn to forgive ourselves in order to move on. Many Christians embrace this idea as well. What does the Bible have to say about forgiving yourself? *Nothing.*

Study the Bible cover to cover, and you will not find self-forgiveness mentioned in precept or by example. However, the Bible *does* teach repeatedly about God forgiving us and that we must forgive one another.

So if self-forgiveness is wrong, why are we still struggling? Robert D. Jones, in his booklet **FORGIVENESS: "I JUST CAN'T FORGIVE MYSELF,"** suggests that our struggle with guilt, shame and regret is a real problem, but calling it something else will never help us out of it. The remedy lies in discovering **why** we feel that way. We must get to what lies at the foundation of our belief.

Webster's defines a fault line not in terms of science, as we did at the beginning of today's lesson. Instead, it defines it as *a split, a rift.*

Gap.

Crack.

Fracture.

What does this have to do with forgiveness? Spiritually speaking, we want to watch out for fault lines in our understanding of God, sin, and forgiveness. We need to be alert for cracks in our foundation—gaps or fractures that could eventually lead to disaster.

**It's time to get to the core of why we can't forgive ourselves. Let's explore some faulty thinking that may be operating in our lives:**

| Fault Lines | Fault Logic |
|---|---|
| We doubt that God has really forgiven us. | We hold a narrow, limited view of God and don't believe the truth that God can forgive even the worst sinner.<br>1 Cor. 6:9-11, 1 Tim. 1:15-16 |
| We do not see our need for forgiveness from God. | We rationalize sin as a "mistake" and underestimate God's hatred of sin.<br>Gen. 39:9, Ps. 51:3-4 |
| We may have never truly entered into God's forgiveness through saving repentance and faith. | We may know the Gospel facts but have never come to Christ on God's terms.<br>Mark 1:15, Acts 20:21 |
| We have a prideful and self-righteous attitude. | *"I still can't believe I did that!"* reveals an underlying issue of pride in which we think we are incapable of such evil deeds.<br>Jer. 17:9, 1 Cor. 10:11-12 |
| We fail to measure up to our own standards of performance or our own image of how good we are/ought to be. | We fail to believe that God is the only One we must please. His law is our sole standard of self-measurement.<br>Phil. 3:7-9 |

*Adapted from Forgiveness: "I Just Can't Forgive Myself" by Robert D. Jones*[1]

**From the chart, do you recognize any faulty logic or fault lines that have been holding you back from fully receiving God's forgiveness?**

 **My "I Get It!" thought for today...**

## Embracing Forgiveness

### Day 3: Root Conditions

Several years ago, our front lawn was peppered with weeds and dandelions. I wanted a beautiful, lush, green lawn. Mowing over them gave us that all-green look we wanted—*for about a day*! It didn't take long for those dandelions to produce another sunny yellow flower. It was going to take more than mowing to solve our problem. We needed to treat the *roots*.

> **Let's pray:** *Father, thank You for the ways You speak to us through nature and ordinary situations. You know all too well the root problems in my heart. Give me the courage to act upon what You show me. In Jesus' Name. Amen.*

Back to our weedy lawn.

I called a lawn service and had them come out and begin treating our grass. That first summer we saw some results; there were fewer dandelions. The year after that it looked even better. Several years later, we have a beautiful green lawn. The process took time. And our lawn continues to need to be treated so that weeds, dandelions, and grubs don't return. The spiritual application for us is obvious:
1. We need to get to the root of the problem to have the results we are looking for.
2. The process takes time.
3. Maintenance is required.

When we've been hurt or wronged, we run the risk of becoming so absorbed in our own pain that we hardly notice how we've hurt others. Or we deny/ignore the real issue and focus on something or someone else as the real source of our problems. That was certainly my personal experience. We may immediately (or eventually) come to see how we've sinned against God, but sometimes that's where it stops. But friend, we must look at our own heart and ask God what He sees.

When we are abused, misused, hurt, or betrayed, our knee-jerk reaction is to protect ourselves against a *next time*. We get angry or subconsciously punish ourselves for believing, feeling, trusting. We go into self-protective mode, shielding ourselves from pain and rejection. But in the end, we only further our struggles. Our hearts get hardened. They get hardened toward men. Hardened toward authentic friendships with women, keeping us isolated and disconnected. Our hearts mistrust the motives of others, and we erect a fortress for protection.

Maybe our heart is hardened toward God too. After all, He failed to protect us in the first place.

A guarded, stony heart says,
 "I don't need anyone."
  "I'll take care of myself."

**What past wound(s) has caused your heart to harden?**




**What past wound(s) has caused you to mistrust God?**

**Look at the illustration below and circle the words that describe the condition of your heart or fill in the blank(s) using your own.**

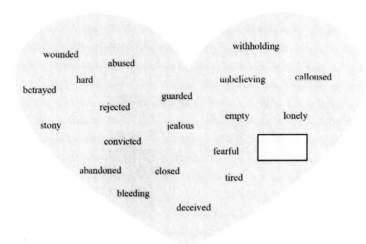

In Jeremiah 2:13, God describes people with a hardened heart toward Him. People who are bent on "taking care of themselves."

Can you relate? In the words of Dr. Phil, "How's that working for you?"

If you remember from my own story, I continually focused on my abortion and how I was hurt. My healing didn't start until I began to see it from God's point of view and how I hurt others. Needing to be healed from my sexual past wasn't even a blip on my radar until I began to take responsibility for my choice to abort. It required a heart checkup.

**Write out the following Scriptures:**

**Hebrews 3:12**




**Ephesians 4:17-19**




The Ephesians passage mentions that they have "lost all sensitivity" and abandoned themselves to all kinds of sin. Make no mistake: *any* of us can lose all sensitivity if we repeatedly ignore the conviction of the Holy Spirit. Webster's defines ignore as *to refuse to take notice*.

**Can you remember a specific time when the Holy Spirit brought conviction to your heart but you ignored Him? What happened to the condition of your heart?**

**Currently, are you refusing to take notice or address an area of your life that the Holy Spirit has been showing you? What has been the result of your choices?**

Having a hard heart keeps us from receiving God's forgiveness and extending it to others. If God is showing you that your heart is hardened toward Him or others, ask Him to exchange your heart of stone for a heart of flesh. **Pray Ezekiel 36:25-27.**

 My "I Get It!" thought for today...

*Embracing Forgiveness*

*Day 4: Prisoner or Party Crasher?*

Today, we'll give attention to two Bible stories in which the characters each needed forgiveness.

**Let's pray:** *Father, I'm more eager to receive Your forgiveness than to give it away. Move boulders in my heart today. In Jesus' Name. Amen.*

**Read Matthew 18:21-35.**

**How do you imprison or torture others who sin against you?**

**Who are you still holding prisoner?**

**In what ways do you expect them to repay you?**

We are often quick to receive God's forgiveness but not so quick to give it to others, especially if they continue to wound our hearts. Peter must have felt that tension too when he asked Jesus, *"...how often should I forgive someone who sins against me? Seven times?"* (vs. 21) The Rabbis taught that forgiveness should be extended three times. Peter, with kind intentions, was willing to give far above what the law required. Jesus' response was *"seventy times seven"* (vs. 22).

**What do you think Jesus meant by His response?**

Let's pause with this thought and go back to something we touched on in Chapter 1. What have you lost as a result of your sexual past? Think about your whole person: physically, mentally, emotionally, relationally, and spiritually. Dig until you can think of 15-20 ways in which you've been affected. ('Cause if we're **in** deep, we need to dig deeper.)

**Write your list here.**

Read the following Scriptures and note what you learn about sexual sin, the impact it has upon oneself and others, and any consequences that will follow. I recommend reading them in a couple different versions of the Bible. Doing so can shed some brilliant light.
Matthew 15:11, 18-19

**Where does sin originate?**

I Thessalonians 4:3-8

**What four things are listed as God's will for you?**
1.
2.
3.
4.

**What warning is given?**

This passage also tells us to "live in holiness and honor." Holiness (or sanctification) means purification of heart and life. Honor refers to a *valuing by which the price is fixed for a person or thing bought or sold*. That price fixed for a person (mankind) was the blood of Christ. Our value is set by God Himself. We must treat others and be treated with that same kind of honor.

**Go back and look at the list of losses you incurred as a result of your sexual past. How many of those same things did each of your sexual partners lose? What did your actions rob them of?**

For 17 years I hurt so badly over the pressure I felt to go through with the abortion. I was eaten up with unforgiveness and was obsessed with blame. And after 17 years, I couldn't take the pain any longer. Hallelujah! My day had finally come! By the gracious hand of God, He opened my eyes and my heart. I finally collapsed under the weight of my burden and recognized my need for healing and forgiveness for the resentment I was holding onto.

During the course of that journey, I had a major revelation. I realized two significant things:

1. Aside from the pressure I felt, I was responsible for the decision I made. God showed me *why* I chose as I did. I finally realized the motivation behind my decision was the very thing that led me into a sexual lifestyle of regret in the first place. (My idols had already been erected.)
2. *My* actions (pregnancy and sexual lifestyle) had hurt my family, as well as my boyfriend and his family.

I immediately felt the burden of sin over my abortion, but sadly, it took 17 years to face my own heart motives and the sin of my sexual past. Sin never hurts just us. It always affects other people. I had hurt God and I had hurt my parents, siblings, boyfriend, and his family. It wasn't all about *me* as I'd thought. As I worked through a Bible study that helped bring healing to my past, I saw with fresh eyes the pain that I had inflicted on others. I finally saw it like God did: I used them as they had me. I had crossed a line and taken something valuable from them.

Part of our sorrow is the painful realization that we had a part to play in our own messy consequences. For many, many years, I experienced a lot of emotions like sadness, anger, confusion, rage, and sorrow. Emotions are real, God-given and part of our humanity. They are like a temperature gauge, revealing highs and lows of the soul. Likewise, repentance is a temperature gauge of the spirit—revealing the condition of the heart.

Herein lays the difference between godly sorrow and worldly sorrow. *The kind of sorrow God wants us to experience leads us away from sin and results in salvation. There's no regret for that kind of sorrow. But worldly sorrow, which lacks repentance, results in spiritual death.* (2 Cor. 7:9-10 NIV).

**Write out Hosea 7:14a for a graphic picture of grief without repentance.**

Let's move into our second story about a woman who is an uninvited guest, a party crasher. This is a story of a woman of ill-repute—the town harlot. What on earth would cause her to cross town and risk embarrassment and ridicule?

**Our story is found in Luke 7:36-50. Go ahead and read it now.**

I can't help but let my imagination take over. Let's put on her sandals for a moment and take a walk with her.

*I wonder...*

Did her heart skip a beat when she learned that Jesus was in her village? Perhaps as she scrambled for her cloak, her eyes fell on one of her most valuable possessions: a bottle of very expensive perfume. Maybe as she walked fast across the village, she stopped just short of the Pharisee's home. Did she think to herself, *"Stop second-guessing yourself! You've come too far to turn back now?"*

*I wonder...*

Did she linger by the doorway, watching as no honor was paid this holy man—Jesus? Is that what provoked her tears? This was the **Messiah**. This was *her* Messiah. Her sins were many, but she was not afraid of Him. He was gentle and His eyes were so kind. She believed who He said He was. With all her heart she believed. And now, she was compelled to do what was in her heart to do. She fell at His feet and wept with gratitude. In her gratitude, she worshipped. She had been forgiven of so, so much. Taking on the role of a lowly servant, she washed the feet of her Lord with tears of joy and gratefulness, wiped them with her hair, and adorned them with kisses of adoration.

*I wonder...*

Were the guests hushed in shocked disbelief? Did they try to quiet her? Did anyone grab her by the arm and try to lift her to her feet? Did anyone call her names, reminding her of her sins? Did anyone perceive her actions as *worship*? Oh, how I wonder...

Her actions were an extravagant display of worship that made those around her quite uncomfortable. All except Jesus, that is. Forgiveness *ought* to provoke a response by the one who was forgiven.

**How have you responded to God's forgiveness? Has it been lavish or limited?**

**Having been forgiven of much, what kind of effect has your forgiveness had on others?**

When the slate is clean and our sins are pardoned, it should make us want to worship God in gratitude for His grace and mercy. But it doesn't stop there. Our response to forgiveness should not only flow vertically in gratitude to God, but horizontally toward others. *Get rid of all bitterness, rage and anger, brawling, and slander, along with every form of malice. Be kind and compassionate to one another, forgiving each other, just as in Christ God has forgiven you* (Ephesians 4:31-32).

Are you ready to hand over the prison keys and let *yourself* go free? Are you ready to crash a party? Risk ridicule? Are you ready to lavish upon Jesus your adoration for His limitless supply of grace and mercy? Go ahead and tell Him. May your praise fill heaven with the sweet aroma of gratitude and worship.

 **My "I Get It!" thought for today is...**

### *Embracing Forgiveness*

### *Day 5: Unlocking Prison Doors*

Yesterday we learned that forgiveness ought to provoke a response in us. That response flows vertically to God as gratitude and worship. It's also meant to flow horizontally toward others not because they are *deserving* of it, but rather because God through Christ forgave *us* (Eph. 4:32). God fully intends for His grace to flow freely through us toward others.

**Let's pray:** *Father, how can I thank You enough for the forgiveness You continually pour out on me? Let me show You by the way I* **live***. Let my life be a fragrant expression to others of the change You have made in my heart. In Jesus' Name. Amen.*

**Write out Matthew 6:14-15**




A dear friend of mine shared the following penetrating thought with me:

Imagine with me that you are in a small room with a cement floor. The walls are made of cement blocks. There's a door. It's locked. The room is cold and damp. So cold. There are no blankets. You can't see anything. There isn't any light or windows. You can't tell how much time has passed in this small cramped place, but you know you've been here a very long time. You are confused, weary, and alone. Completely and utterly alone.

Suddenly, you notice a bit of light seeping in from under the door. Someone is calling out your name, inviting you to come outside. You stand and walk toward the door. As you do, the door opens by itself—not into a hallway, but into an oasis of light and sound and beauty. You squint in the sunlight. Fresh, warm air hits your face. You drink in this goodness. It feels like Life and Love all in one. The light spills into the room behind you. As you turn and look at this room that once held you captive, you notice the walls are embedded with gems and words of love, affirming your worth and value.

You wonder, *"How long has He been calling for me?"*

**How long *has* He been calling for you?**
For a long time, you have been a prisoner of your past. The time has come to unlock those prison doors and be free. The time has come to allow His Light to shine into the corners of that dark chamber that has robbed you of joy and peace for so long.

***The time has come to break loose from that suffocating yoke.***
The time has come to forgive those who robbed you of your innocence, wounded your heart, and broke your trust. The time has come to forgive those who weren't there for you and those who turned their back or a deaf ear to you.

*Are you ready to be free?*

A couple weeks ago you wrote some anger letters. Now you will write a forgiveness letter for every anger letter you wrote. It doesn't mean that they are off the hook or that you can forget all about what they've done. It means that as one who is freely forgiven of her past, you are now offering that forgiveness to others. Forgiveness is not a suggestion; it's a command (Luke 17:4).

**Forgiveness is NOT:**[2]
- *Forgiving and forgetting.* Forgiving and forgetting what someone has done are two different things. We may never forget the sin committed against us by another, but we can forgive them and find peace.
- *A feeling.* Forgiveness is an act of obedience and faith. We will never *feel* like forgiving, but we are commanded to do so.
- *Justifying or excusing sin.* We must acknowledge the sin and how it hurt us. This helps us work through the grieving and healing process. Forgiving someone may take them off of *your* hook, so to speak, but they still have to answer to God.
- *Automatic reconciliation.* If someone has harmed you (as in the case of sexual abuse), and they have not shown remorse or repentance for their sin, they are not a safe person for you or your family to have a relationship with. You can forgive and move on, but don't feel pressured to maintain a connection with them.

**Forgiveness IS:**
- *A choice.* Again, forgiveness is an act of obedience. Feelings will eventually follow.
- *A yoke-breaker.* You may have heard the saying, *"Unforgiveness is like drinking poison and expecting the other person to die."* Unforgiveness keeps us imprisoned to our offender, whereas forgiveness sets us free from their hold on us.
- *The path of every disciple of Jesus.* He forgave those who crucified him even though they didn't ask for it. Christ commands us to do the same (Luke 17:4, Luke 23:34, Colossians 3:13).

**As you prepare to begin writing your letters, look up Isaiah 45:2-3. Trust me, it's a gem! Writing it out helps Scripture to soak into your heart, so take a minute and write it out now.**

That's exactly what God promises to us—gems, treasure—when we break down those bronze and iron gates of unforgiveness. Unforgiveness holds us captive like that cold, dark, lifeless room we imagined ourselves in.

May you find the hidden treasures that He has waiting for you in those secret places as you release these people into the Lord's care. He is calling out to you. How will you respond?

 My "I Get It!" thought for today:

Chapter 9:
Made for Intimacy

# Made for Intimacy

---∞---

*Day 1: Sex, Lies and the Truth*

This week we're going to explore the topic of intimacy. What does it mean to be intimate? Many of us have a jaded perspective of intimacy and limit it to what happens in the bedroom. Sexual intercourse is the most intimate level of physical intimacy that can be shared between a husband and wife, yet sex is not the marker of true intimacy. True, genuine intimacy is so much more than sexual expression.

We can experience intimacy on several levels: sexually, emotionally, and spiritually. Far too often, we try to satisfy our longings for intimacy only in a sexual way. We'll explore what sexual intimacy is not in these next two days and finish the week looking at emotional and spiritual intimacy.

> **Let's pray:** *God, sometimes my head believes that sex is no big deal, but my heart knows otherwise. I don't want my views to be sculpted by the constant dripping of cultural messages anymore. I want the Truth. Help me understand the essence of true intimacy. In Jesus' Name. Amen.*

There is marvelous beauty in God's design. At the dawn of creation, all of God's creation (sex included) was pronounced "good" (Genesis 1:31)—regardless of our personal and cultural views. The *gift* of sex was granted to us for more than pleasure and procreation. There are many great books on this subject that showcase God's design for sex that reach beyond pleasure and procreation.

In this lesson, our aim is to uncover some of the lies that perpetuate our negative views about sex and intimacy.

Our views of sex are formed at a young age. Just as a constant drip of water can sculpt a stone, a constant drip of negative messages about sex can sculpt our views of it. Our views are formed from all sorts of angles: family, friends, church, media, personal experiences, etc.

Unspoken attitudes are just as impacting as those that are spoken. For example, if sex was never talked about in the home, we get the message early on that sex is bad, inappropriate, dirty, etc. If sex is mentioned uncomfortably and quickly during The Talk—*what* we hear and *how* we hear it can speak volumes. Focusing on **sex = pregnancy** gives too small a picture of God's beautiful gift. If we don't understand God's *why wait* and *what for*, then sex becomes just something two people do.

I hope at this point in our journey, you are coming to have a new view of God's design for sex. There's more to come as we continue to chip away at lies that may be lodged in our minds and attitudes of our hearts.

What were your first impressions about sex as a child? Were they positive or negative? As you matured, did sex become something you did to get what you wanted? Was it something you did to get love? What did you come to believe about sex? Like me, were you duped into believing it was something it wasn't? Conned into believing it wasn't what it truly was?

**Write the first thoughts that come to your mind about sex.**[1] Because of the painful experiences of your past, you may have more negative feelings about sex than you do positive ones. Don't despair. God knows. Be honest with Him. Bring the broken pieces of your views on sex and let Him renew your mind and heal your heart.

1. Sex is...

2. Sex is...

3. Sex is...

4. Sex is...

5. Sex is...

> **BIG LIE #101:**
> *"Sex is just sex."*
>
> **TRUTH:**
> Genesis 1:27-28, 31
> 1 Corinthians 6:15-16 NLT

In response to the above statement, I've heard many negative comments from women over the years. *Painfully negative.* My own among them at one time. As you look at your comments again, I pray that you will cry out to God for a deep cleansing in your heart and mind, asking Him to rebuild your attitudes about sex upon His Word.

Satan has a Pandora's box of lies that have been unleashed upon mankind for centuries. But the sexual revolution of the 1960s ushered in a wave of painful and devastating results. Just as the first man and woman believed a lie and *"...the eyes of both of them were opened, and they realized they were naked..."* (Gen. 3:7), we too have fallen for the lie that sex is just an act with little or no consequences other than an unplanned, untimely pregnancy.

Matt Walsh shares:

> "If modern attitudes about sex have 'liberated' us, what precisely, have we been freed from? Security? Commitment? Trust? What, we've broken the Shackles of Purity and Love and run gleefully into the Meadows of Pornography and Herpes? Because that's all that our sexual liberation has wrought. A lot of confusion, a lot of porn, a lot of disease, a lot of emotionally desperate, psychologically battered, spiritually broken people wandering around, searching for another stranger who's willing to go in for a few more rounds of sterile, shallow, pointless sex."[2]

Our culture has fed us a steady diet of "anything goes." If it feels good, do it. What's right for you is not necessarily right for me.

Sex is incredibly bonding, not only physically, but emotionally and spiritually too. We cannot easily break away from a sexual partner and come away unscathed, because every choice we make sexually affects us spiritually.

In 1 Corinthians 6, the teaching about prostitutes and sexual immorality was especially poignant because the temple of the love goddess Aphrodite was in Corinth. Employing more than 1,000 temple prostitutes, sex was part of their worship ritual. Paul was teaching that followers of Christ are to have no part in sexual immorality even if it's acceptable and popular in the culture. Christian author Lauren Winner translates 1 Corinthians 6:16 this way: *"Don't you know that when you sleep with someone your body makes a promise whether you do or not?"*

**In what ways have you bought into the lie that "sex is just sex"? How have your habits and views of sex been influenced by culture?**




**Do you agree with God that sex is "very good"? Why or why not?**




**Write out Hebrews 13:4 MSG:**




Author Dannah Gresh says, "Just like the hippie culture found a pill that conveniently removed the 'inconvenience' of pregnancy, today's hookup culture believes it has found a recipe for removing the inconvenience of emotion: friends with benefits."[3]
Sex without the relationship.
    Sex without the emotional tangles.
        Sex with no strings attached.

> **BIG LIE #311:**
> *"Friends with benefits is better than having no friends at all."*
> *(Hooking up is no big deal.)*
>
> **TRUTH:**
> Hebrews 13:4 MSG

However, scientifically, it just doesn't work that way. Dannah continues, "The brain chemicals associated with romance and sex wash over the deep limbic system during a wide variety of sexual experiences, according to research from the Medical Institute for Sexual Health. Holding hands, embracing, a gentle massage and, most powerfully, the act of sexual intercourse work together to create a cocktail of chemicals that records such experiences deep into the emotional center of your brain. It's why we remember sexual experiences and images so clearly."[4]

In a previous chapter, we learned about dopamine, a powerful chemical in the brain that's released every time you experience pleasure. If something feels good, we want to do it over and over. That's the power of dopamine. And it's how something destructive becomes addictive. So whether you're doing something good for you (like exercising) or bad (doing cocaine), the limbic system gets flooded in dopamine, attaching you emotionally to the source of pleasure. Dannah concludes, "And that's how we become "addicted" and "bonded" to the people we have sex with, even if they are just friends."[5]

So when "friends" no longer share sexual benefits, partners can experience withdrawal symptoms in the emotional center of the brain, which can lead to depression when the source of addiction isn't interested in another hookup.

Matt Walsh asserts:

> "Even the term 'casual sex' is insane. It's an oxymoron. Denim is casual. Restaurants can be casual. CASUAL: without serious intention, careless or offhand, informal. A high-five is casual. Sex can only be viewed in this same vein once we have dehumanized ourselves enough to see human

sexuality as something no more significant than a pair of jean shorts. Describing sex as 'casual' is like describing the ceiling of the Sistine Chapel as a 'nice little doodle.'"⁶

**In what ways have you had a casual attitude about sex?**

Check out BIG LIE #207 in the box. My point in exposing this lie is not concerning contraceptives—to use or not to use. As we know, the purpose of contraceptives is to *prevent* a pregnancy from occurring. But how do we protect or prevent our heart from becoming attached? We can't. The heart becomes attached because it's part of God's design to do so. Sex affects the mind, body, heart and soul.

> **BIG LIE #207:**
> *"Sex is OK as long as you're practicing safe sex."*
>
> **TRUTH:**
> 1 Corinthians 7:2

Matt Walsh contends, "Nameless, random, uncommitted sex is never safe. Not emotionally, not spiritually, not physically. In fact, no sex is safe. Sex is not supposed to be safe. It is supposed to be an act of great depth and consequence. Sex is meant to be open and exposed. It's meant to bring out scary and mysterious feelings of desire and devotion. Call that whatever you like, but you can't call it safe. On the other hand, committed relationships, fortified by the vows of marriage and reaffirmed daily by both spouses, are safe—and it is only in this context that the inherent vulnerability of sex can be made secure and comfortable."⁷

**Write 1 Corinthians 7:2 NLT.**

**In what ways have you kept sex "safe"?**

**Read Genesis 25:29-34 NIV and then write out Hebrews 12:15-17 from The Message.**

Short-circuiting God's path to genuine sexual intimacy for a quick sexual "high" is like Esau trading a lifelong gift to satisfy a short-term appetite.

 **My "I Get It!" thought for today is:**

## *Made for Intimacy*

### *Day 2: The Key to Authentic Intimacy*

Yesterday, we looked at the impact of sexual intimacy. It bears repeating that every choice we make sexually affects us spiritually, emotionally, and physically.

Misusing the amazing gift of our sexuality carries consequences. It reminds me of the time when my sisters and I were just kids. The three of us sneaked into Mom's bedroom snooping for Christmas presents. Imagine our surprise and delight to find out we were getting a bird! We found the cage, birdfeed, and bird toys. The only thing missing was the bird itself. We were so excited! Together, right then and there, we named the bird *Star*. Come Christmas morning, we were excited to meet Star and hear her pretty chirping. But all of our snooping and sneaking actually cheated us out of the genuine thrill of a Christmas morning gift.

God doesn't want us to cheat ourselves by trying to satisfy our longings outside of His design.

**Please hear this: God wants us to experience amazing sexual pleasure and intimacy. His blessing over our bed is poured out in the covenant of marriage.** (More on this in our next chapter.)

There is no other way.

His ways will never change even if popular opinion does.

"But I've already blown it!" We may not be able to return to our virginity again. That was a one-time thing. But whether we're married, single, divorced, or widowed, we can return to purity.

> **Let's pray:** *Lord, restore my heart, my mind, and my purity. Help me to embrace Your ways instead of my own. Following my own ways has only left me empty. Remove the obstacles of indifference and show me what true intimacy looks like. In Jesus' Name. Amen.*

Today, we will look at the emotional impact of sexual bonding outside of marriage. One of the ways sex can impact relationships outside of marriage is by hindering our emotional growth. The emotional level we're at when we begin to have sex outside of marriage is where our emotional intimacy can stall. This can be the hurdle that we find most difficult in getting beyond and the reason why we may feel "stuck" in our marriage, present relationship, or in our relationship with God.

Sex outside of God's design creates a virtual feeling of intimacy. Let's draw on an example from vehicle side mirrors. To prevent lane change collisions, vehicle side mirrors in the USA come standard with a cautionary label that reads:

### WARNING:
**OBJECTS ARE CLOSER THAN THEY APPEAR**

These curved mirrors create a *virtual* image as opposed to a *real* image. This is why we don't see objects in their truest form or with accurate depth perception.

Having sexual intercourse makes us feel close to our partner. However, sex outside of marriage offers only fleeting physical pleasure and a counterfeit form of intimacy. Eventually, we feel empty inside. Anytime we express our sexuality apart from what it was meant to be, we will feel empty.

Using our vehicle mirror illustration, we can say that sex outside of God's design creates a *virtual* feeling of intimacy. If the relationship is centered on sex, it forms a blind spot—keeping us from seeing the red flags in the individual or the potential roadblocks in the relationship.

> **Merriam Webster Dictionary**
> **Virtual:** *very close to being something without actually being it*
> Synonyms: all but, borderline, near, more or less

I don't know about you, but I don't want a relationship that's *more or less* intimate. I don't want it to be *pretty close*, *borderline,* or *nearly* intimate.

I want the real deal.

    I want the real deal in marriage.
        I want the real deal in friendships.
            And I want the real deal with God.

No obstacles.
    No stumbling blocks.
        No *virtual* intimacy.

**Write your own definition of authentic intimacy.**




God has put within each of us a desire for **authentic** intimacy—the desire for someone to truly know us and love us for who we are. Ultimately, only God can fill this craving within our souls. But even still, He blesses us with earthly relationships that do experience the highest levels of intimacy. We call these people our best friends or soul mates.

True intimacy is one of the qualities of a fulfilling marriage, one which we all hope to experience. Sex before marriage may cause us to *feel* intimate—*more or less*—but in reality, it's a false sense of intimacy.

> **Merriam Webster Dictionary**
> **Intimacy:** *a relationship of mutual, honest self-disclosure and acceptance*
> Synonym: belonging, nearness, closeness

Sex is not the indicator of true intimacy.

Wait, what? You might want to go back and reread that statement. To make sure it sinks in, go ahead and rewrite that statement below:

**Sex is not…**

The key to true intimacy is *vulnerability*. Being vulnerable is scary. We want to hide our weaknesses and the not-so-great parts of our character. We hide because we fear that we won't be accepted, liked, or loved if someone discovers "the real me."

So we put on our game face and hide.

But the truth is, we can't have true, authentic intimacy without being vulnerable. We must open up our hearts and be willing to be seen for who we really are. We must begin to trust.

Karlyn Hillerstrom, co-author of **INTIMACY COVER-UP**, notes this about true intimacy:

> "(It) can't be found in arousing each other or being able to sexually excite someone. Anyone can be arousing! True intimacy is when you take off your external shell—the 'you' that the whole world can see –and reveal the reality of the 'you' underneath. It leaves you vulnerable. Opening yourself emotionally to another person takes incredible trust that she or he will accept what you're giving. The potential for heart wrenching pain is off the charts, but without that risk, you'll never find the intimacy you seek."[8]

True intimacy develops when we move from simple conversation with no risk (talking about the weather or sharing thoughts/quotes from a third party) to sharing personal beliefs, as well as our personal story. The desire for intimacy—to connect with another at the highest level of intimacy—has been put within each of us by God. It's at this high level of communication that we risk rejection because we can't change our story.

**In what ways has premarital sex affected where you are emotionally today? (Think about your ability to be emotionally vulnerable with another.)**

**Is it more difficult to be vulnerable with men or women or both? Do you have a best friend with which you can share vulnerably? If not, what do you think is hindering you?**

**In what ways do you react when you begin to feel emotionally vulnerable with others?[9]**
- ☐ Embrace it and share more of myself
- ☐ Clam up and withdraw
- ☐ Change the subject
- ☐ Make sexual advances
- ☐ Make a joke
- ☐ Get irritable
- ☐ Shrug it off
- ☐ Other _____

God knows us at the highest level. He knows the good, the bad and the not-so-great stuff, and He accepts us as we are. Nothing is hidden from Him.

**Read Psalm 139: 1-4. List the things that God knows about you.**

He loves *you*.

If you struggle in the area of relationships—in connecting with your spouse or making friends with others—don't withdraw or hide. Keep at it. Intimacy takes time and an immense amount of trust. Make intimacy with Christ your highest objective, and the rest *will* come. He will teach you.

 **My "I Get It!" thought for today…**

## *Made for Intimacy*

### *Day 3: Rapunzel, Let Down Your Hair!*

This week we've come to better understand what intimacy is and what it isn't. In our next chapter, we'll address more fully the physical aspect of intimacy that God blesses. Today, however, we'll study the barriers to emotional intimacy and how we can overcome them.

Grab a cup of your favorite brew and let's get to it.

> **Let's pray:** *Lord, I keep my heart so hidden at times that even I have a hard time knowing what's in there. But You know me. Lord, You are a strong tower—a safe place for me to hide when I'm afraid. As I hide in You, give me the courage to open my heart to others and risk being known. In Jesus' Name. Amen.*

No one would debate the relational drive of women. Most of us need relationships like we need air to breathe. I'm not talking about finding "The One," but rather the importance of having other women in our lives through authentic friendships. The need to connect with others authentically is part of our DNA; it's there by God's design. We all want someone who "gets us."

Someone who understands our sense of humor.

Someone who trusts our motives and believes the best in us.

Someone who honestly admits when our butt *does* look big in those jeans.

But to be honest with you, I find it difficult to form friendships. Am I friendly? Yes. Am I trustworthy confidante? Absolutely. I love to go deep in conversation, but at the same time, I struggle to get there. Sometimes I find myself camping out in the shallow surfaces of safety, squirming in my own skin. And other times I erect walls to self-protect against exposing my insecurities and inadequacies.

So as challenged as I am to form intimate friendships with other women, I cherish the few that I have.

How about you? Do you struggle to form good, healthy friendships?

Lack of trust is one of the scars left behind by a painful past. We erect walls around our heart because we've been injured by others who shared a secret, leaving us feeling exposed. Or we hide our true selves because we've been misused, abused, or betrayed. Perhaps we steer clear of female friendships altogether because we've been singed one too many times.

We've been burned, so we build. We build tall towers of protection, vowing never to open wide the gates of our hearts.

The movie **Tangled**—Disney's story of Rapunzel—is the tale of a princess who was kidnapped as a baby by the evil Mother Gothel. Having discovered that the infant's golden hair possessed healing powers, the villainess kidnapped Rapunzel and raised her as her own daughter in a tall tower beyond the wood—all the while using the princess' healing powers for her own selfish gain.

For 18 years, Rapunzel believed the lies of Mother Gothel that the world was "a scary dark place" and never ventured outside the tower. While Rapunzel allowed the evil Mother Gothel to use her hair to climb *up* the tower, never once did she consider using her own hair to climb *down* toward freedom.

...That is, not until she decided to pursue her dream. The adventure of following that dream ultimately led to the discovery of her true identity. (Gotta love a princess with a purpose!)

**When you feel hurt, what has been your default reaction? In what ways do you self-protect?**




Like Rapunzel, we may feel trapped in the castle tower of our mind, believing the lies of the past, fearing more rejection, criticism, or judgment. Listening to the debilitating voices of condemnation, insecurity, and pride keeps us locked up in our fortress of mistrust.

Those unseen walls scream, *"Stay back! Don't come any closer!"* Ironically, we *do* want the very thing we often resist, and the intimacy that comes with it, but we're just too afraid of getting hurt. I know, because I had a fortress around my heart for a very long time. It takes trust, vulnerability, and time to bring those walls down.

For most of us, our tendency is to guard our heart by turning inward instead of turning to God. Guarding or protecting is not wrong. Actually, it's quite noble. The issue is ***what*** we're guarding and ***why***.

Scripture clearly identifies several things that are worth protecting. Read the following and note what we are instructed to guard:

**Proverbs 4:13**




**What is the outcome of a person who holds onto instruction (wisdom)?**




**Proverbs 13:3**




**How can guarding our lips (the words we speak) protect us? Our relationships?**




**Malachi 2:14-15**




**God values marriage. Whether you are married or not, in what practical ways can you guard your marriage or future marriage?**

**Proverbs 4:23, Matthew 15:18-19**

**Of all the things we are to guard, Proverbs 4:23 warns,** *"Above all else, guard your heart."* **What do you think we are to guard our hearts <u>from</u>? Why is priority given to the heart? (See Matthew 15:18-19.)**

**How does "guarding our heart" influence our relationships?**

It is clear that there are valuable things we are commanded to guard. We would be fools not to guard our marriages against temptation or infidelity. Nor would we be good parents if we didn't guard our children from negative influences. It just makes good sense to guard those that are most precious.

Let us guard that which is sacred.

We guard instruction (the Word of God) because it's the very thing that teaches us how to live. It's how we know how to discern truth from error—the "everyone-else-is-doing-it-so-it-must-be-okay" kind of messages. We guard instruction because our hearts are prone to stray from Goodness and Truth—leaving us vulnerable to deception from the enemy. And above all, we guard instruction because it's the way we come to know The Lover of our Souls, Jesus.

The more we guard instruction, the more secure we become in His love and the more open and vulnerable we become with others. This is a process that doesn't happen overnight. And while we should strive to be vulnerable with others, the truth is, not everyone is a safe person to do that with. We must learn to distinguish safe people from the Mother Gothels in our lives—discerning who can be trusted with our pasts, our hearts, and our friendship.

From the book **SAFE PEOPLE**, authors Dr. Henry Cloud and Dr. John Townsend identify three characteristics of safe relationships.[10]

Safe relationships are ones that:
1. Draw us closer to God.
2. Draw us closer to others.
3. Help us become the real person God created us to be.

Drs. Cloud and Townsend suggest that a safe relationship is one that *connects*. It's a person who is not just there, but *present* with us. A safe relationship also embodies grace—that quality of unconditional love and acceptance. He/she accepts you right where you are, rather than waiting for you to change in order to be accepted. The third quality of a safe relationship is truth. It involves honesty, authenticity, and living out the truth of God. True safe relationships are ones where we can speak the truth to one another, confronting each other in honesty without condemnation.

Sound like Jesus?

A safe person is one in which we can "let our hair down" and be our real selves.

No pretenses.
  No facades.
    Just the real deal.

A safe person dwells with us in the pit and celebrates with us on the mountaintops. They don't tell us how to feel or think or be. When our feelings are too deep for words, a wise and safe person will draw it out (Proverbs 20:5), accepting us where we are, and pointing us to the Truth.

***We have a responsibility to guard the precious.*** Guard what is yours to guard. And when pain or betrayal come knocking on the door of your heart, offer it to the One who knows it all. Instead of hiding from others and hiding *from* Him—hide **in** Him.

**Write out the following promises:**

**Proverbs 18:10**

**Psalm 32:7**

**Psalm 91:14**

**2 Thess. 3:3**

Beloved, you are not alone. You are worth protecting. Your beautiful heart—every broken or fractured piece of it—is held in His hands. Hiding yourself in Him is not a cop-out; it's an act of great trust. Like Rapunzel, may we *let down our hair*, not for someone else's selfish gain, but because the adventure that awaits just may lead to the discovery of our true identity.

 My "I Get It!" thought for today...

## *Made for Intimacy*

### *Day 4: Ready, Set, Spelunk!*

Jesus is the epitome of a Safe Person. If we're to be known and understood for whom we are, Christ alone must be the source of our identity.

Maybe this is a new thought to you. Whether it is or not, allow me to share a story with you.

Once while my girlfriend Kim was visiting Ohio from her now-home in North Carolina, I wanted to plan an adventure for us. Kim is an adventurer by nature. She often stretches me in this department.

Did I wrestle a bear during my college days? Yes.
Did I bungee jump at will? Yes. (*Sort of.*)

But that all happened when I was in my...well, let's just say it happened a long time ago. I'm much less of the risk-taker than I used to be. But Kim? As I said, she's an adventurer by nature. It's in her DNA. She *lives* for adventure. I, on the other hand, like the *idea* of adventure. Big difference.

So when I considered our big adventure, I came up with what I thought was a great idea. It was something just on the *edge* of edgy—exploring a cave. When I told Kim what I had planned, she nearly squealed. In a sing-song tone, she said, "We're going spelunking!" I quickly retorted, "Noooo! That sounds way too dangerous. We're just going to check out a cave."

A *cavern* to be exact.

While a cave has a large opening at the mouth, a cavern is something that is discovered under the ground. And that's what happened in 1897 on a large farm in central Ohio. The owner of the land discovered a sink hole about 10 feet wide. Over time, that sink hole grew much wider and much, much deeper until the curiosity of a teenage farm hand got the best of him. With a lantern in one hand and a shovel in the other, he began digging. What became of his discovery is known as *"America's most colorful caverns."*

We descended about 60 steps into the mouth of the cavern. I was immediately overcome by the beauty I saw. Beside me, above me, and all around was a spectacular sight of color and unusual formations. Narrow passageways broke off into even more passageways than we were permitted to explore.

God was showing off. I felt His pleasure at my delight.

I wanted so badly to break away from the tour group and linger at every nook, listening for God's whispers in that dimmed place beneath the ground. I was so aware of His presence in that cavern, and He was aware of mine.

He wanted to reveal...
He wanted to teach...

Our tour guide explained that we would descend to a depth of 103 feet below the surface of the ground. Unimaginable! Yet little by little, with every twist and turn, the cavern floor descended until we had indeed reached the cavern depth.

Weeks after my spelunking adventure, I couldn't stop thinking about the cavern. It was during this time (**not** coincidentally) that I had been praying a lot about intimacy—going deeper in my marriage and with the Lord. I came to Him with my questions, fears, and uncertainty.

Then I stumbled upon a worship song that became my mantra for many more weeks. The melody was so beautiful; I couldn't stop listening to it. Part of the lyric from *Fall Afresh* by Jeremy Riddle spoke about how the Spirit of God wanted to blow through the caverns of my soul.

There was nothing coincidental about that! I'm a visual person. Give me truth with a picture and BAM! it sticks. The cavern, full of depth, mysterious beauty, hidden treasures, and undiscovered wonder was a picture of *my soul*. Your soul.

The God of the universe knows every nuance of our soul and wants to blow through, filling it to its fullest measure. There is a deep, cavernous of *knowing* that He wants to happen between us and Him.

We are made for intimacy.
**Sacred intimacy.**

I listened to that song over and over and over again, tears often spilling onto my cheeks. As I prayed for more understanding, He began to connect the dots in my mind and show me His heart about intimacy.

He reminded me about the history of the cavern. It started with a sinkhole. The cavern had been there for hundreds of years, undiscovered. It took the curiosity and commitment of one person to do a little digging, and then the unimaginable happened.

Beauty beneath the mundane.
Holy amidst the humdrum.

That sinkhole was God's **invitation** to discover more of Him. It was an invitation to experience Him at greater depths.

Those places in your soul-heart that are dormant, undiscovered, unfulfilled—He wants to fill with Him. Will you give Him access to those crevices, dark corners, and narrow places to know the joy, unconditional love, and acceptance that you've been craving?

**Write Deuteronomy 4:29**


It is not hard to find Him. He is a God who wants to be found. Remember my story about finding a crucifix in the dirt when I was a 7-year old child?
I found Him in **shallow** dirt.
*Knowing* God (not just knowing **about** Him), is the genesis to experiencing genuine intimacy. He wants depth of mutual discovery to give us hidden treasures, riches stored in secret places (Isaiah 45:3).

Do you want God to blow through the cavern of your soul?
Do you need Him to awaken your soul from its slumber?

We are often like Sleeping Beauty waiting for Prince Charming to waken us to love and life. Yet if we offer the cravings of our soul to the Prince of Peace to be filled, our thirsty souls will be quenched in His love. All others pale in comparison.

There's no shortcut to intimacy with God. It takes vulnerability and risk.

Are you willing to take the risk? Like spelunking, the adventure that waits is full of wonder, beauty, twists, and turns. Sometimes going deeper requires us to face our fears of those dark places. But it is every bit worth it as you uncover the treasures of intimacy in those secret and sometimes less traversed places of the heart.

**Let's pray**: *Lord, the cry of my heart is to be known and loved. And You know me at the deepest level, better than I know myself. Help me to come out of the shadows of fear, take Your hand and discover the hidden treasures in secret places (Isaiah 45:3). In Jesus' Name. Amen.*

## ACTIVITY

God wants to take you on your own adventure with Him that will look quite different from mine or anyone else's. Are you up for the challenge? I hope your heart is beating with anticipation at the thought of going deeper with Christ.

Following are some ways to invite Christ into your leisure activities and increase your intimacy with Him. Choose one from the list below or come up with your own idea. Some of them can be done today. Others may require some planning. Keep in mind that intimacy can't be manipulated or formulated. *It's relational.* Be open to what He wants to teach you through the activity. And *please* don't overthink this. The goal is to remember that God is with you every day, every minute. Invite Him into the ordinary parts of your day, and watch how the ordinary things can become extraordinary moments of intimacy with your Savior.

**Create Art!**
- Paint, draw, color
- Make pottery (or observe a potter at his wheel)
- Play with modeling clay
- Grab your camera. Select a Scripture verse of something that speaks to you and bring it to life through pictures!

**Write!**
- Write a poem about your desire for intimacy with Him, about your healing journey, etc.
- Write a song or a psalm about intimacy. Sing it!
- Cut out pictures from a magazine and write about it. Include how it makes you feel, what draws you to that image, what it says about you, authentic intimacy, etc.
- Free-flow write. Set your timer for 10 minutes and write without stopping. Select a prompt, such as:
  - *Dear Past Me...*
  - *Dear Future Me...*
  - *My Secret Desire is...*
  - *Lord, I want You to know that...*
  - *The three things I'd do if I weren't so afraid...*

**Get Active!**

Is God speaking to you through nature? What is He showing you? Notice what you notice. Talk to Him, ask Him questions, and listen!
- Take a walk or a hike in the park
- Bird watch
- Go spelunking
- Walk the beach or sit and listen to the ocean waves
- Scale a mountain

**Other!** _____

Remember, intimacy isn't developed by using a formula—but by vulnerability in relationship. Whatever you choose, talk to God while doing it. Ask Him to give you eyes to see what He wants to teach you. The point is just to do something that awakens your soul as you connect with God.

 **My "I Get It!" thought for today:**

## *Made for Intimacy*

### *Day 5: Relentless Pursuit*

Earlier in this chapter, we defined intimacy as *a relationship of mutual, honest self-disclosure, and acceptance.* While this definition shows us the mutuality of intimacy, the Biblical meaning of this word gives us deeper insight into the heart of God.

The Hebrew word **yada** (yä·dah') is a word that means *to deeply know.* It is used more than 940 times throughout the Old Testament to describe the kind of relationship God wants to have with His people. For instance, Proverbs 3:5-6 NKJV says:

> *Trust in the Lord with all your heart,*
> *And lean not on your own understanding;*
> *In all your ways ac**know**ledge Him,*
> *And He shall direct your paths.*

This deep knowing that God wants us to have with Him is more than a wink and nod of our head in His direction. But rather a deep-level knowing that can only be shared between those who spend time together.

The word *yada* is also the word used to describe sexual intimacy. We see it in Genesis 4:1 NKJV:

> *And Adam **knew** Eve his wife; and she conceived...*

God uses the picture of sexual intimacy as a holy metaphor. Can you imagine it? The kind of relationship He wants with *us* can be compared to a deeply personal, vulnerable, and private relationship shared between a husband and wife.

> **Let's pray:** *God, how can it be that You desire to be so intimate with Your people? I've been so much like unfaithful Israel. Help me to let go of old cravings and forsake all others. I want to give You my undivided heart. In Jesus' Name. Amen.*

Throughout Scripture, we see the language of God's love portrayed through an unbreakable marriage covenant between a bride (Israel) and her bridegroom (God). Yet we know that throughout Israel's history, she failed to keep covenant with God and chased after other lovers. This He called adultery—often using very graphic language to describe her lewdness. Though Israel broke covenant with her God, God forever remains a Covenant-Keeper.

From Genesis to Revelation, the word covenant is found 332 times. God's covenant—His binding, indestructible, unbreakable agreement—reveals His very nature.

**Look up the following Scriptures and note what you learn about covenant.**

**Deuteronomy 4:13, Exodus 24:7-8**

**What was the covenant? How was it established?**

**Psalm 89:34-35**

**Jeremiah 32:40**

**John 1:14**

**Hebrews 8:6-11**

**Hebrews 9:18**

**Luke 22:20**

**What similarities/differences did you notice between the Old and New Covenants?**

While visiting India as part of my outreach experience with YWAM, our team of 14 people representing five different nations crashed a wedding. (We tried to fit in, but 14 white faces didn't blend in so well.)

We heard the beating of drums and saw several men dancing passionately around a car. *I was enthralled.* I studied each man's face trying to figure out which one was the groom. Just when I thought I'd picked him out of the crowd, the car door swung open and the groom emerged. He was wearing an off-white suit and matching turban on his head. He looked regal. The men celebrating and dancing around him went completely wild with excitement.

As the men continued to dance around him, he slowly made his way to a canopy where his beautiful young bride, wearing an exquisite red sari, and sitting on an ornate chair, waited for him to come to her.

I will never forget that image.

Although these were Hindu people, I saw a picture of Christ in the scene before me. In western culture, we make it all about the bride. But I noticed something beautiful about this eastern tradition:

### *It's about the groom taking a wife.*

*We* are the wife that Christ (our Bridegroom) will one day come and take to be with Him forever. It has always been God's intention for us to be with Him, living together in an unbreakable covenant. Perhaps some of us have a record of breaking promises, breaking relationships, breaking marriages, and breaking hearts. Or maybe you've been on the receiving end of those breakups—afraid to love and trust anyone, even God.

You were made for love.

> An eternity of Love.

**Read the following Scriptures and note God's promises.**

**Isaiah 61:10**




**Isaiah 62:2-5**




**2 Corinthians 11:2.**




My experience in India caused me to do some study on the Biblical Jewish wedding and the parallels to the Church. We're barely going to scratch the surface in our lesson but I encourage you to do your own study on this topic.

**Read Psalm 45:1-15.**
Psalm 45 isn't just a beautiful poem. It's a prophecy of Messiah. From beginning to end, it's the Gospel. One commentary says, "There is no reason to think it refers to Solomon's marriage to Pharaoh's daughter, as some suppose, but rather to Christ and the Church."[11]

In Psalm 45:3-5, the Royal Bridegroom (Christ) is described as a Warrior who is victorious over all his enemies and suggests that this marriage doesn't excuse Him from battle as was permitted by the law (Deut. 24:5), but rather this marriage brings Him *to the battlefield*, for He comes to rescue His bride from captivity. (I don't know about you, but that leaves me weak in the knees!)

In verses 6-9, the Royal Bridegroom is now described as a King and Priest. We see references to Jesus as King and Priest scattered throughout Scripture:

*But about the Son he says, "Your throne, O God, will last forever and ever;*
*a scepter of justice will be the scepter of your kingdom."*
Hebrews 1:8

*Therefore, since we have a great high priest who has ascended into heaven,*
*Jesus the Son of God, let us hold firmly to the faith we profess.*
Hebrews 4:14

The latter verses in Psalm 45 are addressed to the royal bride—The Church, The Bride of Christ. We will look at verses 10-11 only.

**Write out Psalm 45:10-11.**

If you're married, you gave serious thought to your wedding vows. Most likely, you and your spouse promised to...

*love and cherish,*

*in sickness and in health,*

*till death do we part.*

In Psalm 45:10, the conditions (or vow) of our marriage to Christ are: *"Forget your people, and your father's house."*

Does that sound like a wedding vow you would want to make? At first glance, it sounds rude and controlling!

But consider this:

**Could any marriage survive divided affection?**

In the culture of that day, when the groom pledged (engaged) himself to a young woman, he promised to provide for her and love her. He would go back to his village and begin preparing a place for her in his father's house. Then he would return for her and take her to be with him in his father's home.

Waiting for her bridegroom was not a time of inactivity. She was preparing elaborate wedding garments and learning how to be a good wife. She was also preparing for her sacred relationship by mending broken ones.[12]

*But most of all, she was learning to let go.*

A young Jewish bride *had* to learn to let go. After all, she was leaving everything she knew for a place she'd never been to and for a bridegroom she hardly knew.[13]

Jonathan Cahn, author and Messianic Jewish Rabbi says, "The father's house represented her culture and her family, including the ones dearest to her. Forgetting her father's house symbolized laying aside the distractions of everything in it, as well as the claims of her household. She was still a daughter **in** her father's house, but she was no longer **of** his house."[14] She was a bride.

Cahn continues, "Forgetting her father's house included letting go of the messages of her father's house. She had to learn to let go of anything that could cloud her heart and distract her devotion to her bridegroom."[15]

**The messages of our "father's house" can sound like these:**

*"Religion is a crutch."*

*"You're not pretty enough or smart enough."*

*"This is my personality. It's just the way I am."*

*"We don't talk about these things outside this home."*

*"You're damaged. Marked. No one will want you."*

**What are the messages of your father's house that may be clouding your devotion to Christ?**

**What is it that you need to let go of? Fear? Blame? Of thinking that everyone else is "happier" or more deserving than you? Of wrestling with old ways of living?**

Don't long for the empty ways of living, reigniting old flames, or stirring up unholy passions. Be *undivided* in your devotion. Not one foot here and the other one there.
 Just.
  Let.
   Go.

*For your royal husband delights in your beauty;*
*honor him, for he is your lord.*
Psalm 45:11 NLT

The beauty that He delights in is more than a fabulous wedding gown. It's the beauty of her *holiness* with which He is enthralled.

Beautiful One, you know that house that's being prepared for you by your Royal Bridegroom? It's *waaaaaay* better than your father's house because *"...holiness adorns (His) house"* (Psalm 93:5 NIV).

From the time you came to put your trust in Christ, you were learning to let go of old ways of doing things. Even through this Bible study, you've been learning to let go of your secrets, your old ways of living, unforgiveness, and bitterness. It's time to divorce yourself from the worldly ways in which you once staggered and come into your royal position as The Bride of Christ.

Because *nothing* will ever separate you from His love.

He is a Covenant-Keeping God who will *never* break faith with you.

 **My "I Get It!" thought for today:**

Chapter 10:

# He Loves Me, He Loves Me Knot

# He Loves Me, He Loves Me Knot

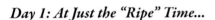

***Day 1: At Just the "Ripe" Time...***

Love songs. There are more of them than we can keep track of. There are classic love songs, popular love songs, extra cheesy love songs, and top love songs of all time. Chances are, you probably have or had a favorite love song at one time—a song that was special just between the two of you. What is it about love songs that make them so special? Love songs are a confession of our emotions for another—a declaration of our commitment. When we love someone, we want the world to know!

This week we'll camp out in Song of Songs, an Old Testament book written by Solomon, who authored more than 3,000 proverbs and 1,005 songs. As far as love songs go, Song of Songs is *the* chart-topper of all chart-toppers.

**Write out Song of Songs 1:1 NLT**

Curious to know what sets it apart? Song of Songs is a wedding song honoring marriage. It's the most spicy and sexy reading you'll find in the entire Bible. It uses sensuous language and explicit statements about sex, but the purity and sacredness of love in this song are much needed in a day when what was declared good in Eden has been perverted, abused, misused, and made all too common and casual.

Solomon was King David's son and the most wise king in the East (1 Kings 4:29-34). Though he was instructed not to marry pagan wives, he did. He took hundreds of women as wives and concubines, most for political reasons. In the end, they led him astray just as God and others had warned him. Are you wondering why God chose Solomon of all people to write a book on marital love and sex when he had so many wives? Not exactly a stellar example. Then again, neither am I. Or you. Maybe that's the point.

Whatever hang-ups we may have about Solomon, let's agree in our hearts to be open to what God wants to teach us through Song of Songs.

Solomon's Song of Songs is a collection of seven poems that features passionate dialogue between a simple Jewish woman and her lover, the king of Israel. This unique song, or poem, provides us with God's blueprint, or master plan, for marriage and sexual intimacy. The two cannot be separated.

My husband, who works in construction, knows the importance of following a master plan when they are setting the steel of a building. The blueprint is detailed. Intricate. One misstep can compromise the entire project.

As we explore the blueprint of Song of Songs, let's turn our hearts to our Master Builder, the One whose foundation is secure.

> **Let's pray:** *Lord, teach me Your ways. I've been following my own plan, my own road map, and it's led to emptiness and brokenness. I need a new foundation. Start first in my heart. Bridge the great divide between my heart and my mind. Make me wholly and holy Yours. In Jesus' Name. Amen.*

Scholars debate over the meaning of Song of Songs. Some argue that it's an allegory about God's love for the Church. Others contend that it's a literal story about married love. Actually, it's both—a historical story with two layers of meaning.

Scholars break down the song into seven poems:
*The Wedding Day (1:1-2:7)*
*Memories of Courtship (2:8-3:5)*
*Memories of Engagement (3:6-5:1)*
*A Troubling Dream (5:2-6:3)*
*Praising the Bride's Beauty (6:4-7:9a)*
*The Bride's Tender Appeal (7:9b-8:4)*
*The Power of Love (8:5-14)*

As we begin examining these poems closely, I recommend reading the passages multiple times in different Bible versions. The unique ways in which some versions word the passage can make all the difference in gaining insight. In addition, notice the words or phrases that seem to stand out to you even if you don't quite understand what it means. God is speaking!

**The Wedding Day**

**Read Song of Songs 1:1-2:7 at least three times.**

In this first poem, the couple reminisces about their wedding day. If it sounds as though there has been some sexual intimacy before their wedding *celebration*—you may be right. But understand this: in Biblical times, the couple would come together under the huppah (a Jewish canopy) where a ceremony would be performed. They would then consummate their marriage in private quarters *before* enjoying a week-long feast with family and friends.

**Record any words or verses that stood out to you in this poem:**

**What character traits did you discover about the woman? About Solomon?**

Solomon and his bride are in love! Words seem to flow easily between them—their feelings, attraction, physical touch—it's all part of their mutual love-talk.

**How does the woman describe herself in 1:5 and 2:1?**

**How does Solomon describe her in 1:9-10, 15 and 2:2?**

Bible commentators concede that the vineyard belonged to Solomon and was leased to the girl's stepbrothers. Busy working for others, she neglected her own appearance, yet she doesn't use negative words to describe herself. In fact, she says in verse 1:5, *"I'm dark, yet lovely."* However, her tanned appearance may have made her feel insecure compared to the fair-skinned women in Jerusalem who were considered much more beautiful. But Solomon loved her dark skin.

**What kinds of words do you use to describe your appearance?**

Lastly, let's consider verse 2:7. Some versions have the woman (Beloved) speaking, in other versions it's attributed to Friends. Regardless of who is speaking, the words are a clear warning:
> *Promise me, O women of Jerusalem, by the gazelles and wild deer,*
> *not to awaken love until the time is right.* (NLT)

> *Oh, let me warn you, sisters in Jerusalem, by the gazelles, yes,*
> *by all the wild deer: Don't excite love, don't stir it up, until the*
> *time is ripe—and you're ready.* (MSG)

Can you hear her pleading? She says, *"Promise me you won't awaken love too soon!" "Let me warn you! Don't stir up love before the time has come!"* I believe she's imploring all of us to look beyond our feelings. Our feelings can make the relationship seem more intimate than it genuinely is. Feelings alone don't make a relationship ripe. There's something more...

Author and Pastor Rick Warren says,

> "Today we've bought into this myth that love is uncontrollable, that it's something that just happens to us; it's not something we control. In fact, even the language we use implies the uncontrollability of love. We say, 'I fell in love,' as if love is some kind of a ditch. It's like I'm walking along one day and—bam!—I fell in love. I couldn't help myself.

"But I have to tell you the truth: That's not love. Love doesn't just happen to you. Love is a choice, and it represents a commitment. There's no doubt about it: Attraction is uncontrollable, and arousal is uncontrollable. But attraction and arousal are not love. They can lead to love, but they are not love. Love is a choice."[1]

**How much emphasis do you or have you placed on attraction and arousal in building a relationship? Explain.**

In verse 2:7, **The Message** uses the word **ripe** to describe the time of sexual love. As one who worked in a vineyard, the woman would have known all too well when the grapes were ripe for harvest. Those that had reached their peak would taste the sweetest and make the best wine. On the other hand, I'm sure she had tasted the bitterness of fruit that had been picked too soon.

The Beloved's marriage and sexual union with Solomon provoked inspired words not only for those within her sphere of influence, but for generations of people throughout the ages—including me and you. Personal experience doesn't always have to be the teacher. We would spare ourselves so much grief if we would heed warnings such as hers. Maybe it was her devotion to Yahweh that kept her pure. Or perhaps she had one too many girlfriends cry on her shoulder who had stirred up love too soon, reaping a harvest of tears, broken hearts, underdeveloped intimacy, and a bitter aftertaste.

**What kind of "fruit" did you harvest as a result of your sexual past?**

**If you had an opportunity to influence others about waiting for sexual love until the time is "ripe," what would you say?**

 My "I Get It!" thought for today:

## He Loves Me, He Loves Me Knot

### *Day 2: Blossoming Vines*

Today we're going to look at the second poem in this seven-poem series. Remember to read it at least three times in different Bible versions if at all possible.

**Memories of Courtship**

**Read Song of Songs 2:8-3:5**

After a harsh winter, people everywhere are invigorated by the first signs of spring. Birds sing creation's song. The air smells clean and fragrant. New colors burst onto the landscape. Animal life awakens from their drowsy slumber.

In this poem, the couple share memories of their courtship. It's springtime in Israel, and Solomon wants to experience the wonders of spring with the woman he loves.

**Record any words or verses that stood out to you in this poem:**




**Looking over what you just wrote down, what do you think it means?**




In Israel, springtime marked the season for the blossoming of the grapevine. The NASB says, *"The time has arrived for pruning the vines..."* (2:12). Pruning a vineyard involves cutting away every vine that doesn't have a blossom on it. At this stage of growth, there aren't any *visible* signs of fruit—only the *promise* of fruit. The purpose of pruning is to provide the buds or blossoms with as much of the sap and sunlight as possible. Cutting away barren, superficial, or sickly branches directs nourishment to the healthy parts of the vine, enabling it to produce fruit.

So what's pruning got to do with love? A lot actually.

I believe God is giving us a picture of a relationship that starts out like most others: with budding attraction. Without question, Solomon and the Shulammite woman are attracted to one another. But as we looked at yesterday, attraction is not love. And arousal is not love. A relationship built on attraction and arousal alone creates a shaky foundation.

The *"blossoms on the vines"* are a picture of their developing love. Blossoms produce fruit, and their relationship has the **potential** to bear much fruit. However, it's their choice if they will pick the fruit prematurely or allow time to prune their relationship.

**What kind of fruit is produced within a relationship built on attraction or arousal alone?**

**If pruning involves cutting away barren, superficial or sickly branches, what does "pruning" within a dating relationship look like? Or within a marriage relationship?**

**In your past, how did a lack of pruning in your relationships spoil the vine?**

There's even more serious implication to the pruning process. Pruning is essential for an abundant harvest, but the weather also has a direct effect on the ultimate harvest. Not only does it have a direct impact on that year's harvest, but it also dictates the *following* year's crop. The message to us is this: the decisions we make early in a relationship will affect the "harvest" of the relationship in the future, as well as future relationships. We can harvest bitter, emotionally underdeveloped fruit in our relationships, or bear sweet, ripe, and mature fruit. If a relationship resists being pruned, how well does it endure the harsh storms of life?

**What are some of the storms of life that relationships face?**

**Write out Songs of Songs 2:15**

In The Message, this verse is attributed to Beloved. She says, *"Then you must protect me from the foxes, foxes on the prowl, foxes who would like nothing better than to get into our flowering garden."*

**What do you think she is asking of Solomon?**

**What are the foxes that can destroy a relationship?**

**In closing this poem, write out Song of Songs 3:5.**

**In the NLT, verse 3:5 is attributed to Friends or the Daughters of Jerusalem. How open have you been to friends or family speaking truth or warnings about a relationship you were involved in? Why or why not?**

 **My "I Get It!" thought for today:**

## He Loves Me, He Loves Me Knot

*Day 3: A Garden of Delights*

As a little girl I liked to play bride. I don't remember having a special dress, but I do remember using a tissue atop my head as a veil! I would march around with a fistful of wilted flowers, imagining a handsome man waiting for me.

**If you are unmarried, have you imagined what your wedding day might look like? Explain.**

**If you are married, what was your wedding day like? Do you remember the feelings you had about your groom and the life you would share together? How did you feel about yourself?**

Today, we're going to examine the third poem: The Wedding Procession (3:6-11), The Wedding Night (4:1-5:1) and Consummation of the Marriage (4:16-5:1). Whether you're married or single, the message of this Song is for you, so take it to heart.

**The Wedding Procession, Wedding Night & Consummation**

**Read Song of Songs 3:6-5:1 in at least three different versions if possible. Record any words or verses that stood out to you:**

**Song 3:6-11** specifically address the wedding procession. What a vision King Solomon must have been with his army of valiant men at his side. Scripture often leaves out the details that I crave—leaving my imagination to kick into overdrive! However, in a scene like this, all of my senses are engaged. I can almost smell the exotic spices, see the beauty and splendor of Solomon's chair, and hear the grunting of the camels or horses as they kick up dust, proudly escorting the king as he comes to claim his bride. Call me a hopeless romantic!

**What feelings does this scene provoke in you?**

**Song 4:1-15** gives an intimate and private account of their wedding night. In the passion of their love, they praise each other with beautiful poetic imagery.

**What does Solomon praise in his bride? What character traits does he praise in her?**




**Does Solomon equate sex with love? Explain why or why not.**




*You are my private garden, my treasure, my bride, a secluded*
*spring, a hidden fountain.*
Song 4:12 NLT

*You are a garden locked up, my sister, my bride; you are a*
*spring enclosed, a sealed fountain.*
Song 4:12 NIV

One of the things Solomon praises in his bride is her purity. Until that time, she was *"a garden locked up...a sealed fountain."* She had waited until the time was ripe for sexual love. Solomon describes her garden as a paradise of rare spices (NLT) and succulent fruits (MSG).

**How does the bride respond to her husband? Read Song 4:16. What do you think she's talking about?**




In the previous poems, she warned others not to awaken love before the "ripe" time. But now she's singing a new song. Her garden is her virginity—her sexual love. In the MSG she declares, *"Let my lover enter his garden! Yes, let him eat the fine, **ripe** fruits."* Allowed to linger on the vine, the fruit of their love has reached its peak in the marriage bed.

All of this talk about gardens and fruit makes me think about another couple in the Bible: Adam and Eve. You know the story, but let's mine for hidden gems.

**Read Genesis 3:1-16.**

God placed Adam and Eve within a beautiful garden that God Himself walked in (vs. 3:8). He granted them to eat fruit from the trees in the garden, except from **one** tree. From the very beginning, we see that God had some restrictions with His people that were for their very best.

The woman *"saw that the fruit...was good for food and pleasing to the eye...and she ate it. She also gave some to her husband, who was with her and he ate it. Then the eyes of both of them were opened, and they realized they were naked; so they sewed fig leaves and made coverings for themselves."* (Genesis 3:6-7)

If you've ever been judgmental of Eve (as I have), it's time for an attitude check-up. Sister, our desires are the **same** as hers: she felt like she was missing out on something.

**What did you think you were missing out on when you agreed to engage in consensual sex?**

To Eve the fruit on the tree *looked* good. How about you? Have certain individuals looked good on the outside? They *say* the right things. They may even *do* the right things most of the time. Maybe you thought the circumstances of your meeting were too bizarre, too coincidental to be anything but God's will.
So we take the bait and we eat it. We eat and are left with a bitter aftertaste. Our eyes are opened.

> Open to shame and suspicion.
> > Open to distrust and doubt.
> > > Open to blame and brokenness.

We reaped a harvest of consequences we weren't counting on.

For Adam and Eve, their beautiful Garden of Eden became a place of shame and hiding. The garden didn't change. It was still beautiful and life-giving. God's presence still dwelt there. But the introduction of sin brought change. Sin changed the way they viewed themselves. It changed the way they viewed God and each other. They were afraid and hid.

Not only is our sexuality a garden—a sacred place, but Scripture says that our bodies are also a temple (1 Corinthians 6:19). For many, our garden seems anything but sacred. It's become a wasteland through abuse or misuse—a place of shame. God wants to reclaim your garden and make it a sacred place. We can't reclaim our virginity, but we can reclaim our purity. The marriage bed can be made pure for you and your spouse. If you're not married, your garden can become a sacred place again when you allow the fruit of your sexual love to linger on the vine until it's reached its peak in the marriage bed. God has a promise for those who believe He can make streams in the wasteland. Do you believe?

**Read Isaiah 43:19 and turn it into a prayer to God.**

 **My "I Get It!" thought for today:**

## He Loves Me, He Loves Me Knot

*Day 4: The King is Enthralled with your Beauty*

Today we're going to look at poems four and five in our seven-poem series. Since all scripture is useful for teaching, rebuking, correcting, and training in righteousness (2 Timothy 3:16), let's ask ourselves, *"What does God want to teach me in this? Am I holding to any views of marriage or singleness that need corrected?"*

**A Troubling Dream**

**Read Song 5:2-6:3 in at least three different versions of the Bible if possible. Record any words or verses that stood out to you in this poem:**

The marriage between Solomon and his bride grew and matured over time. Whereas she had enjoyed the pleasures of sex in their relationship, it now seems the woman's attitude is dramatically cool and cavalier toward her husband's sexual advances.

**If you are married, has your attitude about sex with your spouse become cool and cavalier? What do you think are the contributing factors?**

One contributing factor can be the thoughts we allow our minds to dwell on. Married or not, if we focus on the shortcomings of others, that's all we'll see. If you've ever been caught in this web, then you know that these destructive thoughts don't automatically shut down when you lie down. Many a night did my negative thoughts pick up speed when what I really needed was sleep. I felt like the Shulammite when the night watchmen found her as they made their rounds: *beat up*. Yes, our thoughts can beat and bruise our attitudes toward one another, keep us in disunity, and affect our sexual relationship with our spouse. If we're not careful, these negative thoughts can lead us to an emotional or physical affair as we focus on the proverbial greener grass of another relationship.

**How do you talk about your spouse to other people? Do you use positive or negative words? Do you focus on the things he doesn't do or the things he does? If you're not married, how do you talk about other people?**

For those who are unmarried, it may not be negative thoughts that are beating you up, but rather the obsession over men, marriage, and relationships. Our desires for love and relationship are instilled by God and were meant to cause us to seek Him first for fulfillment. In Him alone are we truly satisfied. Apart from Christ, our desires become dictators of our identity. Beloved, let us offer up our legitimate desires to God alone. God will dethrone everything that tries to usurp His place. There will be no other god before Him (Exodus 20:3).

**In what ways have obsessing over men, marriage, and relationships become dictators of your identity?**

Often if things have been a little cool, we want our man to make the first move toward us. But maybe **you** need to be the one to make that first move. Observe the Shulammite's example. She wasn't stingy with her words. Her words flowed freely as she described her husband. In so doing, her heart was drawn back to him just as strong as before.

**What are some things she admires in her husband Solomon in verses 10-16?**

**If you're unmarried, what are some qualities that you are looking for in a spouse?**

**If you're married, what are some things you admire in your husband?**

I encourage you to tell your spouse what you admire in him. Write him a love note or share it with him in private and see what happens (*wink-wink*).

Let's turn a bit of a corner and look at the sixth poem from Song of Songs.

**Praising the Bride's Beauty**

**Read Song 6:4-7; 9a in at least three different versions of the Bible if possible. Record any words or verses that stood out to you in this poem.**

In this poem, Solomon responds to his wife, describing her beauty and the things he loves about her. **What does Solomon praise about his wife?**

Solomon sure had a way with words, didn't he? Starting at her sandaled feet and moving to the top of her head, Solomon is generous with his praise. Though he did have many wives and concubines, Solomon made it clear that *"there's no one like her on earth, never has been, never will be. She's a woman beyond compare"* (6:8 MSG).

While her beauty was undoubtedly extraordinary, Solomon praised her inner beauty as well when he exclaimed, "*Your beauty, within and without, is absolute*" (7:6 MSG). Both Solomon and his wife praise one another for their inner beauty, proving that it's not just something that women should possess. Phrases like, "*milk and honey are under your tongue*" (4:11 NIV) and "*your mouth is like the best wine*" (7:9 NIV) are indicators of an inner beauty.

**What do you think milk, honey, and wine represent?**

Our inner beauty is revealed through the words we speak to ourselves and to others. Jesus made this point in Matthew 15 when He said that all kinds of evil come from the overflow of our hearts.

I truly believe that every woman is uniquely beautiful despite how Hollywood, magazines, or the scale define it. Most of us have never won a beauty pageant and never will. However, there is something that is winsome beyond all else. Write out the following verses and commit them to memory.

**Proverbs 31:30**

**1 Samuel 16:7**

Friend, it isn't your personality, likability, your fashion sense, or what the scale says. It isn't your intelligence, your education, social status, marital status, or bank account. It isn't your skill set, the car you drive or the "toys" you have that draws Christ to you. It's Christ **in** you that radiates an inner beauty that is beyond compare. Oh yes, the King is enthralled with your beauty (Psalm 45:11).

**Ask the Lord to tell you what He finds beautiful in you. Write down what He tells you.**

 My "I Get It!" **thought for today:**

## He Loves Me, He Loves Me Knot

*Day 5: Like a Seal on Your Heart*

Here we are at the end of our week-long study on the Song of Songs, and I hope it's stirred some things in your heart about God's blueprint for marriage and sexual intimacy. Today we'll look at the final two poems in the seven-poem series.

**The Bride's Tender Appeal**

**Read Song of Songs 7:9b-8:4 at least three times. Record any words or phrases that stood out to you.**

In *Memories of Courtship* (the second poem), it was springtime in Israel, the vineyards were in bloom, and love was in the air. In this sixth poem, the language indicates that the couple has been married for some time.

As a marriage develops, both partners should develop with it, growing in love and freedom. After having "cooled" in her attitude toward sex with her husband, the woman has quickly turned it around, even initiating sex with her husband.

**Have stereotypes in lovemaking hindered you from initiating sex with your spouse? How do you feel about initiating sex?**

In this poem, it's springtime again, and the blossoming vines point to the time of pruning. Marriage, like the blossoms on a vine, endures times of growth that come when wise couples prune back distractions, busyness, and other things that may drain the relationship from developing as it should. Making our marriage priority over everything else (second *only* to our relationship with Christ) will produce *"choice fruits, both new and old"* (7:13 NASB).

**What do you think "new and old choice fruits" could mean in your relationship whether you're married or not?**

**Write out Song 8:4.**

**What do you think her purpose is in repeating this phrase?**

## The Power of Love

**The seventh and final poem is found in Song of Songs 8:5-14. Read it at least three times in different versions if possible. Record any words or phrases that stood out to you.**

In verses 6-7, the young woman gives a passionate discourse on the power of love that is recited in many modern-day weddings. She begins, *"Place me like a seal over your heart, like a seal on your arm."* A seal in biblical times was used to guarantee security or indicate ownership. The signet is a hard emblem that can only make a deep impression on soft substances like clay or wax. In verse 6, she is pledging her fidelity to her husband and asking Solomon for the same. In essence she's saying, *"Our love is deeply impressed on our hearts. Forever, it's me and you and no other!"*

She continues, *"...for love is as strong as death, its jealousy unyielding as the grave. It burns like blazing fire, like a mighty flame. Many waters cannot quench love; rivers cannot wash it away. If one were to give all the wealth of his house for love, it would be utterly scorned."*

**She identifies some powerful characteristics of love. What are they and what is she saying about them?**

One of the characteristics of love that she points out is jealousy. Jealousy and envy are twisted sisters. Like me, you probably hold the belief that jealousy has a negative connotation. And it *does* if the object of our jealousy doesn't belong to us.

In its most positive sense, jealousy means *to be filled with righteous zeal.* Let's apply this definition to the topic at hand: **LOVE**.

**Is it appropriate to be jealous <u>over</u> one's spouse? How does it differ from being jealous <u>of</u> your spouse?**

**Write out the following Scriptures:**

**Exodus 34:14**

**Deuteronomy 32:16**

**2 Corinthians 11:2**


**What makes God jealous?**


**In what ways have you aroused God's jealousy?**


**Write out Ephesians 1:13.**


When you trusted Christ as your personal Lord and Savior, you were sealed with the Holy Spirit. You bear His image and are under His authority. God's sealing is never forced. You become His by choice, and His imprint is formed within you. A seal can only leave a deep impression on soft substances like clay or wax, not on hard substances like stone or metal. Spiritually, Christ's impression can only be left on a soft heart of humility, not a hardened, prideful heart.

The last half of this final poem seems to turn a sharp corner on the subject of marriage and relationships. But in reality, it offers helpful advice from the ancients.

In Song 8:8-10, the girl considers days when she was younger and under the charge of her brothers who were probably responsible for helping her prepare for marriage one day. They decided if she stood firm like a wall against sexual temptation (remained a virgin), they would praise her. But if she was open to immorality (like a door), they would intervene. In 8:10 she testifies that her purity and virginity are intact and thus found favor in Solomon's eyes.

Through your journey, you now have a rich understanding of God's design for marriage, sex, and relationships. God has given you a voice to share these truths with others in your sphere of influence—children, grandchildren, friends, co-workers, and church family alike.

1. For those standing firm like a wall against temptation – PRAISE THEM and encourage them. Women and men need to know that not everyone is "doing it." They are not weird or odd for wanting to wait until marriage for sex. Express your respect and pleasure in their decision. Honor them.
2. For those in your life that are a "door"—who have been opened to immorality—pray for opportunities to speak God's truth in a non-judgmental way. Just because you've blown it doesn't disqualify you from being God's messenger. On the contrary, you know full well the pain and anguish that immorality has caused in your own body, mind, soul, spirit, and relationships. You now possess a key that can unlock prison doors and set captives free!

 **My "I Get It!" thought for today:**

# Chapter 11:
# Unchained Melody

# Unchained Melody

*Day 1: Band-Aids, Balm, and Satan's Big Lies*

When I was a child, my mother was the one I ran to for comfort. She hugged and kissed me and bandaged my skinned knees. Whatever pain I felt just melted away with her tender hug. As I got older, my wounds looked different. Kisses didn't make them feel better anymore. And there weren't enough Band-Aids in the world to fix the pain in my heart. But that didn't stop me from trying to cover up the pain with something or someone. Can you relate? I *know* you can relate. Your heavenly Father knows the things you've run after to make the hurt go away. Hear His cry for you:

> My dear Daughter—my people—broken, shattered, and yet they put
> on Band-Aids, saying, *"It's not so bad. You'll be just fine."*
> But things are not *"just fine!"*
> Jeremiah 8:11 MSG

**Let Jeremiah 8:11 be the basis of our prayer today:**

*Father, my heart has been broken, and in many ways, my life is shattered. You alone are my cure, and with Your strength, I won't return to lame remedies. On the outside, I've tried really hard to make it look as though things are "just fine." But You know better. Apart from You, there is no healing. I trust You. Break off these ties that bind me, Lord. In Jesus' Name. Amen.*

Sweet friend, you've come so far on this journey. You are nearing the end of a painful passage, and you see light at the end of the tunnel. You're beginning to feel joy and breakthrough. Lies have been revealed, and truth is proving to set you free. Gone are the Band-Aids that disguised your painful wounds. Hallelujah! Christ has come with the soothing balm of His Word and healed your wounds.

**That's why you don't want to overlook this crucial next step in your healing process by permanently severing the unholy sexual soul ties that have kept you bound.** So be aware of Satan's big lies such as #841.

> Though you may be feeling good—great, even—don't settle for that. When feelings subside, you want the assurance of having taken it to the Cross. You want permanent severing of those soul ties so you can have permanent healing. Accept nothing less.

**Preparing to get FREE:**

First, you will need the list of sexual partners that you've been working on since Chapter 4. If it is not complete, you'll need to finish it before moving on. Then, come to the Lord with a humble heart. Ask Him for eyes to see your sin the way He does. He alone is your Deliverer.

Allow yourself adequate time to pray through your list. Don't be rushed. You will have two days to complete this assignment. Don't put it off until tomorrow. You will need time to pray through your list.

> **BIG LIE #841:** *You don't really need to do this. You've got all the freedom you need. You're feeling pretty good, aren't you?*

- **F—Find** a quiet place where you won't be disturbed or distracted.
- **R—Reflect** on God's amazing love and His desire to set you free.
- **E—Exercise** your faith, believing He is willing and able to sever the ties.
- **E—Entreat** the Lord. (Pray!) Ask Him for eyes to see things the way He does.

As you entreat the Lord, ask Him to reveal every unrighteous sexual use of your body with each person on your list. Revealing it (bringing it from darkness into Light) is the work of the Holy Spirit. Our part is to renounce the sin. Renouncing is a formal or definite way of saying that you refuse to follow, obey, or support (something or someone) any longer.

In his book, **HELPING OTHERS FIND FREEDOM IN CHRIST**, Neil T. Anderson lists the following types of unrighteous sexual uses of the body that should be renounced:[1]

- Premarital sex
- Extramarital affairs
- Homosexual sex
- Pornography (books, magazines, movies, videos)
- Sexual perversions and compulsive behavior (inordinate sexual appetite, masturbation, sexual fantasies, anal/oral sex, devices)
- Prostitution (heterosexual and homosexual)
- Sexual perversions (bestiality, sadomasochism, transvestitism, trans-sexuality)
- Pedophilia (sexual preoccupation with young children)
- Rape (any sexual use of one's body by someone without consent)
- Child sexual abuse or incest (molestation)
- Abortion
- Sexual spirits (*incubi* and *succubi*)

> **Ask the Lord to reveal every unrighteous sexual act with each person on your list. Pray something like this:**[2]
>
> *Lord, reveal to my mind every sexual use of my body as an instrument of unrighteousness. In Jesus' Name. Amen.*
>
> **As He reveals, renounce each incident:**
>
> *Lord, I renounce <u>(the act)</u> and the unholy bonds it created with <u>(the person)</u>. Lord, forgive me for sinning against You and against my own body. In the name of Jesus, sever the soul tie that was created with this person physically, emotionally, and spiritually. I present my body to You as a living sacrifice, holy and acceptable to You, reserving the sexual use of my body for marriage only.*
>
> *I renounce the ways that Satan has perverted my attitudes toward sex, men/women, and myself because of my sexual past. I claim the truth that I don't have to keep living as a victim of my past experiences. Thank You, Lord, for Your power to totally cleanse and forgive me.*
>
> *In Jesus' Name. Amen.*

So how about Big Lie #949? Though you may not *feel* different, believe me, you **are** different! My friend, it's ALL changed. If it weren't, Satan wouldn't try so hard to convince you otherwise. Trust in the Lord and His promises—not your feelings (Prov. 3:5-8 NLT).

> **BIG LIE #949:** *Nothing's changed. I don't feel any different.*

 **My "I Get It!" thought for today:**

## Unchained Melody

> **BIG LIE #613:** *You don't have to finish this now. You can always come back to it later.*

### *Day 2: Plowing the Path to Freedom*

Yesterday, you began praying through your list of sexual partners, believing God to sever those unholy ties of your past. Today, you will pray through the rest of your list.

Satan is not your friend. He will do everything he can to distract you and keep you from permanent healing. Don't give into the idea that you can come back to it later when you feel like it. Usually, that feeling doesn't come!

*"Don't put it off; do it now! Don't rest until you do. Save yourself like a gazelle escaping from a hunter, like a bird fleeing from a net* (Proverbs 6:4—5 NLT).

Once again, find a quiet place where you can have uninterrupted time with God. Come humbly before Him.

**Pray the following prayer[3] (or one like it) by asking the Lord to reveal every unrighteous sexual act with each person on your list.**

> *Lord, reveal to my mind every sexual use of my body as an instrument of unrighteousness. In Jesus' Name. Amen.*
>
> **As He reveals, renounce each incident:**
>
> *Lord, I renounce <u>(the act)</u> and the unholy bonds it created with <u>(the person)</u>. Lord, I ask Your forgiveness for sinning against You and against my own body. In the name of Jesus, sever the soul tie that was created with this person physically, emotionally, and spiritually. I present my body to You as a living sacrifice, holy and acceptable to You, reserving the sexual use of my body for marriage only.*
>
> *I renounce the ways that Satan has perverted my attitudes toward sex, men/women, and myself because of my sexual past. I claim the truth that I don't have to keep living as a victim of my past experiences. I claim the truth that I don't have to keep living as a victim of my past experiences. Thank You, Lord, for Your power to totally cleanse and forgive me.*
>
> *In Jesus' Name. Amen.*

As you close for today, soak in the promises of restoration from Isaiah 49:9-10 NLT. He IS the pathway to freedom. In His mercy, He leads us out of bondage and into a place of abundance, safety, and refreshment.

> *I will say to the prisoners, "Come out in freedom,"*
> *and to those in darkness, "Come into the light."*
> *They will be my sheep, grazing in green pastures*
> *and on hills that were previously bare.*
> *They will neither hunger nor thirst.*

*The searing sun will not reach them anymore.*
*For the LORD in His mercy will lead them;*
*He will lead them beside cool waters.*

**Go ahead and love on Him. Journal your joy and gratitude.**

 **My "I GET IT!" thought for today:**

## Unchained Melody

### *Day 3: Going AWOL*

In order to break free and *remain* free, it will take making healthy choices. Tough choices. It'll require breaking free from unhealthy people, unhealthy influences, and unhealthy habits. It'll take going AWOL on your past.

AWOL is a term that means *Absent Without Official Leave*. In military terminology, leaving without permission is the same as desertion or abandonment. One who deserts her post or duty without permission does so with the intention of not returning.

Going the way of the world promised us passion without pain, sex without strings, love without commitment, and control without compromise. Along the way, we've unintentionally "enlisted" ourselves into bondage. And the war we've been battling has been ruthless and merciless at times.

Are you ready to go AWOL on your past?

Are you ready to abandon your post of imprisonment once for all?

By praying through your list of sexual partners, you have broken the spiritual and emotional bond that was created with each of them. Now it's time to deal with physical reminders of our past. Things like letters, jewelry, photos, etc., can trigger memories of past sexual partners and keep the bond, or attachment, alive.[4]

Taking this step can be hard to do. Maybe the hardest. It's not easy ridding one's life of the physical reminders, but I believe it's part of the process that God honors.

There were times in Israel's history when they were permitted to keep the plunder after a battle. Other times, they were not to take anything for themselves because it was *devoted to destruction* (Joshua 7:12). I don't entirely understand the connection that physical reminders have on us emotionally and spiritually, but God does. After God told Joshua that there was sin in the camp, He told Joshua to tell the Israelites, *"Consecrate yourselves in preparation for tomorrow; for this is what the Lord, the God of Israel, says: There are devoted things among you, Israel. You cannot stand against your enemies until you remove them"* (Joshua 7:13).

Consecrate means *to set apart for sacred use*. If we're going to stand against our enemies, we have to do things God's way.

**Consider going AWOL from the following four categories of physical reminders:**

**A—Apparel:** This includes clothing, jackets, intimate apparel, etc. that were received as gifts.
**W—Words:** This includes notes, cards, letters, emails, texts and contact information from past lovers.
**O—Objects of Significance:** This includes jewelry, photos, music, and other gifts that were received from past lovers. (Wedding photos of an ex-husband should be handled wisely. Consider passing them on to your children.)
**L–Literature:** This includes books, poetry, etc. that were received as gifts.

**Pray about each category and ask the Lord to show you if there is anything in your possession (or tucked away in a basement or attic) that He wants you to abandon.** (There may be other things that are not listed that God shows you.)

**Write them down here:**

**What will you do with these items? And when?**

If this is especially difficult to do, ask a friend to hold you accountable. I have led many groups through this process. I have seen women give clothing and jewelry to other members in their group. Both were thrilled in their own way: an act of obedience by one and a joyful recipient by the other!

**As we close here for the day, look up Psalm 37:39-40 MSG and note what "the free life" offers us:**

 **My "I Get It!" thought for today:**

## Unchained Melody

### *Day 4: Guard this Command*

Yesterday, we learned that being healthy starts with going AWOL on physical reminders of our past. Coming clean allows us to *be* clean. As we abandon physical reminders of our past, we also want to examine behaviors and learn to set healthy boundaries that will keep us living and remaining free.

The book of Proverbs was written by Solomon, who was not only King of Israel, but a father to sons and daughters alike. Solomon was the son of King David by Bathsheba. You probably know their story, which is found in 2 Samuel 11-12. I can't help but wonder that David must have passionately prayed for, warned against, and instructed his sons about the dangers and destruction of adultery. David knew firsthand the painful consequences of such sin. And now Solomon, son of David, had his own sons. Proverbs 7 chronicles his impassioned plea to avoid such a path.

> **Let's pray:** *Lord, I'm prone to wander from You. My heart wants to thrive in You, but my flesh seeks its own satisfaction. Your words are life. Today, I choose to store them up within me so that I will live. In Jesus' Name. Amen.*

A proverb is *a short, concise statement that conveys moral truth.* They are considered self-evident truths, a "no-brainer."

Except God knew better.

While the proverbs (and entirety) of God's Holy Scripture stand as truth, He knew we would need to be reminded over and over again of certain things. He warns against the sin of adultery and sexual immorality more than **100 times** throughout Scripture. God desperately wants us to get this point: sexual immorality—any sex outside of God's divine plan—binds us to our detriment.

Proverbs 7 is written as a warning against the adulteress and seductress. Although this advice is directed toward young men, young women should take note as well. You may have been the seductress in your past or the one that was seduced. Either way, we have much to learn if we are willing to hear its message. It clues us in to Satan's strategies to destroy our purity, our marriages, and our testimonies. But we are not unaware of his schemes (2 Corinthians 2:11). Storing up God's Word within us and yielding to God is the key to victory over sexual temptations.

**Have you used your sexuality to seduce another? If so, what do you think was your driving force? What need did it satisfy in you?**

**Read Proverbs 7.**

*Guard this command* **(Prov. 7:1, 5):** We're to guard this command/teaching like we would guard our very eyes. Our eyes are sensitive. They are sensitive to bright light, extreme temperatures, and foreign objects like dust, debris, make-up, etc. Our eyes are also sensitive to what they *see*. We have learned how visual images play an important role in the bonding process.

Sexually charged books, explicit R-rated movies, not to mention pornography, can stimulate wrong desires and cause our hearts to stray, so *guard my teachings as the apple of your eye* (Proverbs 7:2). Get rid of the visual junk.

**What are you exposing your eyes to?**

*Among the simple* (**Prov. 7:7**): The youth who lacked judgment was not alone. He was surrounded by other young men. The writer of this proverb calls these young men "simple." The Hebrew word for simple means *foolish* or *open-minded*, as in *one easily persuaded and enticed*.

Our culture highly values an open mind. Be careful that keeping an open mind does not entice you into a lifestyle that ensnares. Choose your friends wisely. *Bad company corrupts good character* (1 Corinthians 15:33).

**Make a list of your friends. Prayerfully evaluate them. Are those in your circle of friends drawing you toward Christ or away from Him?**

*Strategies of seduction* (**Prov. 7:10-21**): We can discover five characteristics of a wayward woman from these verses. (Keep in mind that these truths are for men too.)

1. <u>She's dressed like a prostitute (vs. 10)</u> – I'm not sure how prostitutes dressed in biblical times, but apparently their clothing gave them away. I really don't intend to step on any freshly pedicured feet, but ladies, our clothing shouldn't give *us* away. The mystery of modesty is sexier than flaunting our assets, leaving nothing to the imagination. Revealing more than we ought to **doesn't** make one a prostitute. Be careful not to give someone a wrong impression of who you *really* are: a daughter of God.

    **In what ways have you dressed to get noticed by others?**

2. <u>She's a smooth talker (vs. 21)</u> – Our wayward woman had all the right moves. She was honey-tongued and knew just what to say to get what she wanted. Any voice of resistance was drowned out by her loud and persuasive words. She won't take "no" for an answer.

    **Have you ever been seduced by a smooth talker? How or what did he/she say that hooked you?**

    **Have you ever used smooth and persuasive talk to get what you wanted?**

3. <u>She's got attitude (vs. 11-12)</u> – This woman is defiant and rebellious. The Message version says she's "*brazen and brash, restless and roaming, never at home, walking the streets, loitering in the mall, hanging out*

*at every corner in town.*" Even in my teen years, I knew this kind of person was nothing short of trouble. Lacking direction and purpose, she is on her own path and doing her own thing without regard for others. If we're not careful, we can be well into our adult years and caught up in the same destructive patterns.

**Do you see a pattern in your life of being in places you shouldn't be? Explain.**

4. <u>She has crafty intentions (vs. 12)</u> – This gal was lurking at every corner. The Message puts it this way: (the woman had been) *lying in wait for him, dressed to seduce him.* The term "lying in wait" gives me a mental image of something being hunted. When a hunter has his prey in view, his gaze is locked-on-target. The hunter is sneaky. Stealth. And the prey is always unsuspecting.

Social media and online dating can be a fun way to connect with people. But the shadow side is its great potential for people to hide their true selves, to lurk or lie in wait for unsuspecting bait. Not everyone has the best of intentions.

**What boundaries do you need to put in place to maintain healthy relationships online or in person?**

**In what ways have you been lured by the crafty intent of others? In what ways have you used crafty intent in your relationships?**

5. <u>She's persuasive (vs. 13)</u> – She's not only persuasive with her words like we identified in #2, but this gal is persuasive in action. She's bold but not in a courageous way. *She took ahold of him and kissed him* (vs. 13). She's a person who lacks boundaries and self-control.
We can't live a life that is holy and whole if we have relationships with people who don't respect sexual boundaries.

**What boundaries do you need to put in place to keep yourself holy and whole?**

Whether you have been the Seducer or the Seduced, this can be a tough message to hear. If we really want to change the course we're on, it'll take soul-searching and being honest with ourselves. For honesty to reap a harvest, it will require making some changes in the way we pursue dating and love relationships. The Holy Spirit will show you truth and empower you to walk in His ways so that you *"will live"* (Prov. 7:2).

 **My "I Get It!" thought for today:**

## Unchained Melody

*Day 5: Walking in Freedom*

Before we finish this week, I want you to take a little Before-and-After Inventory. Think back to how you felt at the very beginning of this journey. How would you describe your feelings and your views about sex, yourself, others, and God? Consider where you are at this point in your journey. How would you describe your feelings and your views now?

| HOW I FELT WHEN I STARTED | HOW I FEEL NOW |
|---|---|
|  |  |

Feel like celebrating yet? You've worked hard and come a long, long way. You probably feel different in many ways. And you may see things—many things—differently. All along the way, God has been celebrating over every step of faith you've taken and every act of trust you've shown. Go ahead and give yourself a little **woo-hoo!**

The feelings of peace, joy and freedom you're experiencing are real. I have seen countless women transformed by the Word of God as they applied His truth to their wounds. It's a transformation filled with hope and joy for a new future. Sin has been forgiven and forgotten. We are no longer weighed down by secrets and shame. We find peace *with* God and are restored by the peace *of* God. And all this time, Beloved, He never let go.

**Do you have any fears about moving forward outside the accountability of this group experience? Explain.**

**How can you make sure you keep walking in freedom after this Bible study ends? Read and write out the following verses:**
- **Psalm 119:45**


- **James 1:25**

**What do these verses mean to you?**

We know when we are free because the effects of our freedom are undeniable. Likewise, we know what it's like to be enslaved to something. Slavery is defined as *submission to a dominating influence.* Ever been dominated by food? Alcohol? Emotions? Lustful passions and the like? Look again at your descriptions in the Before-and-After Inventory. Your slavery was evident even though you might not have called it such. Freedom, on the other hand, is *liberation from slavery or restraint or from the power of another.* Simply put, freedom means *life*!

**Write out Galatians 5:1:**

**Read Romans 6:15-18 from The Message and write it out in your own words.**

> **BIG LIE #248:** *This time (or relationship) is different. I'm stronger now.*

In both of these verses, we learn much truth. At the core is that **old ways don't work**. However, Satan will try to convince you otherwise. You have an adversary who wants to kill, steal, and destroy your testimony, freedom, and joy. If we want to live in freedom, we will have to walk in the Light of His Word.

 **My "I Get It!" thought for today:**

# Chapter 12: Unbound

# Unbound

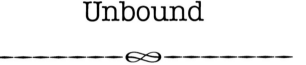

### *Day 1: At Death's Doorstep*

You did it! You've nearly crossed the finish line on this leg of your healing journey. As the weeks have gone by, you may have come to realize that there is more work that needs to be accomplished in your heart. Don't let that discourage you. Receive the promise that *he who began a good work in you will carry it on to **completion** until the day of Christ Jesus* (Phil. 1:6). Enjoy the freedom you are experiencing and remain open to God's leading when He is ready to take you deeper.

As we wrap up our study this week, we will revisit the dynamic true account of the raising of Lazarus found in John 11. In so doing, I believe we'll discover that we have more in common with Mary, Martha, and Lazarus than we may have thought.

**Read John 11:1-45.**

Although Mary and Martha sent word to Jesus about Lazarus' illness, Jesus didn't come. As we know, He stayed where He was another two days. We can take His delays or unanswered prayers as lack of care or love. But we know better than that by now, don't we?

Jesus knows something that these sisters do not.

>There is a bigger plan in the making.

>>A bigger purpose about to be revealed.

**During your journey these past weeks, in what ways have you come to find Jesus in your past?**


### *Finally, he said to his disciples, "Let's go back to Judea." But His disciples objected.* (John 11:7—8 NLT)

The disciples objected because Judea held certain danger. The Jews had tried to stone Jesus a short while ago, and now Jesus wanted to go back there? But Jesus was never afraid to face dangerous situations to rescue those in darkness.

The place of healing you are now experiencing is because you had courage to face your own Judea—a place of fear and uncertainty. However, like those early followers, we often object to the places Jesus wants to take us on our healing journey. We doubt His ways and question His goodness.

**What "places" in this journey did you object to going? Check all that apply.**

- o   Sharing your story
- o   Writing out your Sexual Background List
- o   Writing anger letters
- o   Naming and grieving your losses
- o   Discerning your heart motives
- o   Extending forgiveness to others
- o   Praying and breaking the soul ties of your *entire* Sexual Background List
- o   Being vulnerable with others
- o   Getting rid of reminders from the past
- o   Other _____

**What made you object to these specific paths along your healing process?**


**Write a prayer of thanks for the friend(s) who encouraged you along life's journey in general and/or your present healing journey. Thank God for seeing you through the checkpoints you "objected" to but are now reaping the benefits of healing.**

 My "I Get It!" thought for today:

## Unbound

### *Day 2: A Bigger Plan*

We've all heard the saying, "Hindsight is 20/20." In other words, it's only after we come through the circumstance at hand that we can see it clearly—making any sense of it. And still, there are events in our life that will never make sense. We must trust El Roi—*The God who Sees*—and rest in His heart of goodness toward us, believing that He will cause all things to work for the good of those that love Him (Romans 8:28).

In John 11, Mary, Martha, and Jesus' disciples needed fresh eyes of faith to receive what Jesus was about to do.

> Let's ask God to open our eyes: *Father, help me to see Your bigger picture. There is no rewind button for life; no delete button to forget those things that have brought much pain. Give me fresh eyes of faith to trust Your heart toward me today and in all of my tomorrows. In Jesus' Name, Amen.*

**Read John 11: 1-45. Write out John 11:14-15.**

Jesus finally reveals the mystery of His delay: "*...so that you may believe.*" The Lord doesn't withhold His hand from a situation just to make us squirm. His delay always serves a purpose. There is a bigger picture at play—one that brings our deliverance and His glory.

In this chapter, Jesus uses the words *believe/believes* **six** times. The repetition of the word is meant to grab our attention.

**What do you think the Lord may be asking you to believe about your sexual past? About your future?**

*When Martha heard that Jesus was coming, she went out to meet him, but Mary stayed home.* (John 11:20)

When we're hurting, somehow we trudge through time—one awful day at a time. We go through the motions of daily routines, fluctuating between denial and despondency. Maybe that's why Mary *stayed at the house* while Martha went to meet with Jesus. The ESV says, "*...but Mary remained seated*" (vs. 20).

Think back to the example in Chapter 1 about the football game between rival teams: It's the 4th quarter and the score is tied. Your team has the ball at the 5-yard line with just seconds remaining. The noise level in the stadium is deafening. All eyes are on the field. The ball snaps and everyone is out of their seats.

That is, all except Mary. *She remains seated.*

She's *unmoved.*

**Is there anything remaining in your sexual past that is keeping you *un*moved?**

*Martha said to Jesus, "Lord if You had been here, my brother would not have died."* (John 11:21 ESV)

Perhaps Mary and Martha muttered dozens of times, *"This isn't the way Laz's story was supposed to go. This isn't how his story should have ended..."* We've likely have thought the same thing about our own story.

Martha asks, *"Lord, if..."*

IF. A tiny two-letter word that packs a punch.

Her question is often our question. We may think to ourselves, *"This isn't how I thought my story would go. If only I could rewrite that chapter of my past, I would do it differently next time."*

Only we can't edit the pages of our past, can we? Regrettably, we can't rewrite those ugly chapters of our lives—the ones that include adultery, abuse, incest, or addiction.

After spilling out her disappointment to Jesus, He says, *"Your brother will rise again."*

Martha answers, *"I know..."*

How quickly our *"if only's"* turn to *"I know's!"* How many of us casually say, *"I know..."* to truth that we really need to hear or follow but tend to ignore? If our actions aren't lining up with our *"I know's..."* then we need to reevaluate what we **really** believe.

> *Jesus said to her, "I am the resurrection and the life. He who believes in Me will live, even though he dies; and whoever lives and believes in Me will never die. Do you believe this?* ( John 11:25-26 NIV)

Like a skillful surgeon, Jesus cuts to the heart of the matter: *"Do you believe?"*

Jesus introduces Himself by a new name, but it went unnoticed by Martha. To the woman at the well, He revealed Himself as Living Water. To those who were hungry on the hillside, He was the Bread of Heaven. And now, to a grieving sister, Jesus revealed Himself as The Resurrection and The Life.

**In what ways have you experienced Jesus as The Resurrection and The Life? What has He resurrected from the dead in your life?**

**By what name have you come to know Jesus through this journey of healing?**

**In what areas of your life do you still need His resurrection power?**

 **My "I Get It!" thought for today:**

# Unbound

## *Day 3: Overcoming If-Only*

Jesus is unafraid of our questions—the ones we've asked out loud and the ones lodged in our hearts that haven't yet found words.

As you've been discovering, He alone can bring purpose from our pain. And because His Word is timeless, the true account of Lazarus' raising in John 11 has a message for me and you.

**Read John 11:1-45.**

> **She called Mary aside from the mourners and told her, "The Teacher is here and wants to see you. Now Jesus had not yet entered the village, but was still at the place where Martha had met Him." (John 11:28, 30 NLT)**

This time when Mary hears that Jesus is near, she rises quickly to meet Him. Scripture specifically points out that Jesus did not enter the village but stayed at the place where Martha met him. Jesus does not go anywhere He's not been invited. He possesses the power to heal, but He wants to be invited into your circumstance, your situation, your grief.

When Mary meets Jesus, not surprisingly, she brings the same question (or accusation) that her sister Martha did:

> *"Jesus, if only You had been here...."*

Those that surrounded Mary and Martha also came with their blazing accusations: *"He healed others, couldn't He have kept Lazarus from dying?"*

Our sincere questions can be the spark that sets the whole forest ablaze with doubt and mistrust in God. And even in our profound healing, there may be those who will question where God was in our ordeal—wondering why we even had to experience heartbreak or pain in the first place.

**How will you respond to those kinds of questions? How will you silence the critics?**

**Are there any questions about your sexual past that you are still seeking God for answers?**

> ***When Jesus saw her weeping, and the Jews who had come along with her also weeping, He was deeply moved in spirit and troubled...Jesus wept. (John 11:33, 35 NIV)***

The NLT says that *"a deep anger welled up within Him, and he was deeply troubled."*

**Why do you think Jesus was angry?**

I think that Jesus may have been angry at the consequences of sin. Death was **never** part of His plan. The consequences of sin had brought unbearable pain, sadness, and separation.

Not only did He experience anger over this death, but He also joined in their grief and wept. One commentary suggested that Jesus wept not because Lazarus was dead, but rather He wept over the people's hopelessness.

Jesus experiences strong emotions over each of us. He is *moved* by the sin that has separated, entangled, and consumed us for so long. His grief moved Him to action. That's precisely what compassion is. It's not just feeling sorry for someone, but rather being **moved to action** on behalf of another. It's what took Him to the Cross for us.

**How does it feel to know that Jesus wept at Lazarus' tomb? Do you believe He cries over every injustice that you've experienced? How does that change the way you view your past?**




We can't go back and undo what has been done. But my prayer is that we've found a Mighty God who can cause us to be at peace with our past and restore to us the years that the locusts have eaten. (Joel 2:25)

No more licking our wounds.

No more shame that devours our sleep, our trust or our peace.

In its place is the quiet assurance from the Prince of Peace who has worked a miracle in our hearts and repaid our brokenness with dignity, honor and hope.

**Close today with a prayer of gratitude for the ways in which God has caused you to be at peace with your past.**

 My "I Get it!" thought for today:

# Unbound

## *Day 4: Take Away the Stone*

Lazarus was placed in a cave that had a large stone laid across the entrance.

**LIFE** and **DEATH** separated by a boulder.

Some of us have felt a boulder-size weight upon our shoulders for most of our lives because of the wounds from our past. But now that weight has become lighter and lighter, and you are standing straighter and stronger! As we continue our study of John 11, let's ask God for wisdom and understanding:

> *Father, thank You for the burdens that You have lifted from my shoulders and my heart. You truly are my Burden-Bearer. Give me wisdom and understanding to keep true to Your path of freedom and peace. In Jesus' Name. Amen.*

*"Take away the stone," He said. "But Lord," said Martha, the sister of the dead man, "by this time there is a bad odor, for he has been there four days." (John 11:39 NIV)*

Oh, to hear the gasp that must have echoed in the village when Jesus told the people to take away the stone! But to see the miracle, the obstacle needed to be removed. And in order to experience our own miracles, we needed to remove the obstacles that kept us separated from having an *abundant* life in Christ.

The obstacle of unbelief.

The obstacles of pride and rebellion.

The obstacles of idolatry and secrecy.

**What obstacles have you removed from your life to experience your breakthrough and healing?**


**Read John 11:39 and note how many days Lazarus has been dead: _____**

Again, Scripture gives us specific details about events and times, and yet at other times, it leaves more questions than it gives answers. But in this verse, we know very clearly that Lazarus has been dead four days. Not just dead for days—but dead FOUR days.

Four days is a short amount of time, but it can become significant when we consider what can occur within the body without food or water—how much more so when the body is without **life**! After death, rigor mortis sets in within 2-12 hours, and the body begins to putrefy within 36-72 hours.

Martha objected to Jesus' request to remove the stone. Likewise, we sometimes object to exposing the decay of our past to the Light of Truth. When Martha objected, in essence she was saying that Lazarus' case was helpless and hopeless. When bones are dried up, we are ready to admit that all hope is lost. Suggesting that Lazarus could not be raised to life again only put more glory upon Christ who did it!

**Is there anything that you thought was dead or hopeless in your sexual past or in your present circumstances that Jesus has raised to life?**

> *...He cried out in a loud voice, "Lazarus, come out." The man who had died came out, his hands and feet bound with linen strips, and his face wrapped with a cloth. Jesus said to them, "Unbind him, and let him go."*
> (John 11:43—44 ESV)

Lazarus—a DEAD MAN—*responded* to Jesus' voice. A man whose body was decaying and putrifying beyond recognition—hopeless and helpless—responded to The Resurrection and The Life. When we invite Christ into our helplessness, He is spurred to compassion and action.

*"Take off the grave clothes and let him go."*

**Write out John 11:44b using your name instead of "him."**

**You** responded to His voice. In the dark tomb of your brokenness, you heard the Voice of One who spoke the universe into being call out your name. And *you* came forth. You came forth into Light.

Love.

    Mercy.

        Truth.

            Grace.

                Wholeness.

                    Freedom.

Those grave clothes of shame, guilt, bitterness, and rejection that have kept you wrapped up and bound have been loosed by Jesus—The Resurrection and The Life.

You are UNBOUND!

Jesus didn't only command the onlookers to unbind Lazarus, but also to *let him go*!

    He was released from death unto life.

        From captivity to freedom.

So now, you too are unbound and free to go—free to have joy, purpose, love, and an abundant life in Christ.

**In praise to God, tell Him how you feel now as opposed to when you began this journey.**

## Unbound

### *Day 5: God is My Help!*

Several times throughout Scripture, the Israelites are told to gather stones of remembrance. These Ebenezer Stones marked God's help and victory and literally meant, *"Thus far has the Lord helped us."*

As we put the final exclamation mark on our amazing healing journey, you will create one final collage, just as you did in Chapter 2. This collage will be an Ebenezer Stone of sorts that declares, *"Thus far has the Lord helped me!"* It will put a voice to how you feel about yourself and your past NOW. This is an extremely rewarding exercise, so please don't bypass it.

## ACTIVITY

> On a piece of poster board, create a "View-of-Yourself NOW" Collage. Use pictures and words from a magazine to illustrate how you see yourself and your past NOW.
>
> Give yourself a time limit. Don't overthink it. If you're doing this study with others, be prepared to share your collage with the group.

### *Now for one concluding thought...*

Interestingly, Lazarus' name means **GOD IS MY HELP**. The meaning of his name sounds similar to the meaning of an Ebenezer. The Jews would have known all about the Ebenezer stones. When the Israelites were ready to cross into the Promised Land, 12 men were appointed to take up a stone upon their shoulders—one for each tribe of Israel. These stones were to serve as a sign or a witness among them, so that *"In the future when your children ask you, 'What do these stones mean?' tell them that the flow of the Jordan was cut off before the ark of the covenant of the LORD...and are to be a memorial to the people of Israel forever"* (Joshua 4:1-7).

The memorial wasn't for God. It was for the *people* so that they would remember God's mighty deliverance, power, and provision. Throughout the ages, these stones that could tell tales stood as witnesses to God's might.

When Jesus resurrected Lazarus, he became a **living stone** of God's miracle-working power—a **living** witness. No more would the stones of earth bear witness to God's help. Jesus would enable people—walking, talking, breathing people—to be His living stones to proclaim His marvelous grace!

*You are His living stone.*

The story you have to tell speaks of a God who relentlessly loves, pursues, heals, and claims you as His own.

Sweet friend, there is purpose for your life. Purpose for that pain you endured.

**Write out John 11:45.**

As you traveled this difficult road, others *have seen what Jesus did* (John 11:45). Through the valleys and the peaks, all eyes have been watching. Your testimony bears witness to God's amazing grace and power to heal and restore.

**Write out Psalm 107:1-2.**

**Name three people you plan to share your amazing story with this week:**
1.
2.
3.

*Father, words cannot express the freedom I feel and the thankfulness in my heart for the darkness that You have released me from. Help me to live the rest of my days unbound. Let my life be a living stone that bears witness to Your glorious grace!*

*In Jesus' victorious Name. Amen!*

# Endnotes

**Chapter 1: Good Mourning**
1. Eldredge, John and Stasi. <u>Captivating: Unveiling the Mystery of a Woman's Soul</u>, page 59. Thomas Nelson, Nashville, TN. Copyright 2005.

**Chapter 3: Hearing From God**
1. Dawson, Joy. <u>Forever Ruined for the Ordinary: The Adventure of Hearing and Obeying God's Voice</u>, page 17. YWAM Publishing, Seattle, WA. Copyright 2001. Used by permission.
2. Ibid, pages 45-54.
3. Ibid, pages 59-71.
4. Ibid, pages 71-81.
5. Ibid, pages 81-86.

**Chapter 4: Search & Rescue**
1. DeMuth, Mary. Mary DeMuth's Blog: <u>God Can Heal Your Past</u>. March 4, 2013. <u>http://www.marydemuth.com/?s=god+can+heal+your+past</u>.
2. Eldredge, John and Stasi. <u>Captivating: Unveiling the Mystery of a Woman's Soul</u>, page 26. Thomas Nelson, Nashville, TN. Copyright 2005.
3. Ibid, pages 47-48.
4. Ibid, 49-50.
5. DeMuth, Mary. Mary DeMuth's Blog: <u>God Can Heal Your Past</u>, March 4, 2013.
6. Cochrane, Linda. Adapted from <u>Pathway to Sexual Healing</u>, pages 39-40. Baker Book House Co. Copyright 2000.
7. Warren, Rick. <u>Daily Hope with Rick Warren: Start the Healing by Revealing Your Hurt</u>. May 21, 2014. <u>http://www.rickwarren.org/devotional/english/start-the-healing-by-revealing-your-hurt</u>.
8. Wilson, Barbara. Adapted from <u>Break Free</u>, pages 42-43. Lightning Source, La Vergne, TN. Copyright 2009.

**Chapter 5: Masters of our Demise**
1. Though not quoted directly, the information in this chart was taken from <u>Pulling Back The Shades</u>, by Dannah Gresh and Dr. Juli Slattery. Pages 61-63. Moody Publishers, Chicago, IL. Copyright 2014. . Used by permission. Original work by Dr. Joseph Dillow.

2. Though not quoted directly, the questions to consider when discerning gray issues came from <u>Pulling Back the Shades</u> by Dannah Gresh and Dr. Juli Slattery. Page 65. Moody Publishers, Chicago. Copyright 2014. <u>Intimate Issues</u> by Linda Dillow and Lorraine Pontus. Waterbrook Press, Colorado. Copyright 1999. Used by permission.
3. DirtyGirlsMinistries.com http://dirtygirlsministries.com/?page_id=6597.
4. FamilySafeMedia.com. http://familysafemedia.master.com/texis/master/search/.
5. McIlhaney, Jr., Dr. Joe S. and Dr. Freda McKissic Bush. <u>Hooked: New Science on How Casual Sex is Affecting our Children</u>, page 33. Northfield Publishing, Chicago, IL. Copyright 2008.
6. National Campaign Survey. 2008 Polling Data. http://thenationalcampaign.org/resource/sex-and-tech.
7. Chapnik, Randi. <u>Mom Faze</u>, February 6, 2013. http://momfaze.com/whats-a-little-sexting-between-adults/.
8. Lewis, Monika. <u>The Truth About Emotional Affairs</u>. Focus on the Family. http://www.focusonthefamily.com/marriage/divorce-and-infidelity/affairs-and-adultery/truth-about-emotional-affairs
9. McBurney, Louis. <u>Today's Christian Woman: Is Masturbation a Sin?</u> August 2013. http://www.todayschristianwoman.com/articles/2013/august/is-masturbation-sin.html.
10. Slattery, Dr. Juli. <u>Today's Christian Woman: Guidelines for Christian Sex</u>. October 2013. http://www.todayschristianwoman.com/articles/2013/october/christian-sex-guidelines.html.

## Chapter 6: The Smoldering Embers of Anger
1. Adapted from Counseling Center Village. www.ccvillage.buffalo.edu

## Chapter 7: Shedding the Grave Clothes of Shame
1. http://counsellingonstirling.com.au/understanding_shame.html
2. Ibid
3. Ibid
4. Warren, Rick. <u>Daily Hope with Rick Warren: Practice the Principle of Replacement</u>. May 21, 2014. http://www.rickwarren.org/devotional/english/practice-the-principle-of-replacement.
5. Holcomb, Justin and Lindsay. <u>Rid of My Disgrace</u>, page 73. Crossway Publishing, Wheaton, IL 60187. Copyright 2011. Used by permission.
6. Ibid, page 73.
7. Ibid, page 75, 79.

## Chapter 8: Embracing Forgiveness
1. Jones, Robert D. Adapted from <u>Forgiveness: "I Just Can't Forgive Myself."</u> P&R Publishing, Phillipsburg, New Jersey. Copyright 2000.
2. Wilson, Barbara. Adapted from <u>Break Free From Your Sexual Past</u>, page 148. Lightening Source, La Vergne TN. Copyright 2009.

## Chapter 9: Made for Intimacy
1. Cochrane, Linda. <u>The Path to Sexual Healing</u>, pg. 54. Baker Books, Grand Rapids MI. Copyright 2000.
2. Walsh, Matt. The Matt Walsh Blog: <u>Abstinence is Unrealistic and Old Fashioned.</u> *http://themattwalshblog.com/2013/11/09/abstinence-is-unrealistic-and-old-fashioned/.*
3. Gresh, Dannah. http://religion.blogs.cnn.com/2011/05/31/my-take-there%E2%80%99s-nothing-brief-about-a-hookup/.

4. Ibid
5. Ibid
6. Walsh, Matt. The Matt Walsh Blog: Abstinence is Unrealistic and Old Fashioned. http://thematt-walshblog.com/2013/11/09/abstinence-is-unrealistic-and-old-fashioned/.
7. Ibid
8. Hillerstrom, Karlyn and P. Roger Hillerstrom. The Intimacy Cover-Up: Uncovering the Difference Between Love and Sex, page 37. Kregel Publications, a division of Kregel, Inc. Grand Rapids MI. Copyright 2004.
9. Ibid, page 35.
10. Cloud, Dr. Henry and Dr. John Townsend. Safe People, page 143. Zondervan, Grand Rapids MI. Copyright 1995.
11. Matthew Henry Commentary on Psalm 45. http://www.blueletterbible.org/Comm/mhc/Psa/Psa_045.cfm.
12. Cahn, Jonathan. The Mystery of the Bride and the Bridegroom. https://www.youtube.com/watch?v=zs7IW4luyb4. 1999.
13. Ibid.
14. Ibid.
15. Ibid.

## Chapter 10: He Loves Me, He Loves Me Knot
1. Warren, Rick. Daily Hope with Rick Warren: Love is a Choice. May 21, 2014. http://www.rickwarren.org/devotional/english/love-is-a-choice_498.

## Chapter 11: Unchained Melody
1. Anderson, Neil T. Helping Others Find Freedom in Christ, page 220. Regal Books (A division of Gospel Light), Ventura CA. Copyright 1995.
2. Ibid, page 219, 222—223. Adapted.
3. Ibid.
3. Wilson, Barbara. Break Free From Your Sexual Past, page 181. Lightening Source, La Vergne, TN. Copyright 2009.

# Additional Resources

**After-Abortion Care**
*Forgiven & Set Free*
By Linda Cochrane

*Portraits: Unveiled Freedom*
By Fern Buzinski

**Recommended Reading**
*Boundaries: When to Say Yes, How to Say No, to Take Control of Your Life*
By Dr. Henry Cloud and Dr. John Townsend

*Captivating: Unveiling the Mystery of a Woman's Soul*
By John and Stasi Eldredge

*Forever Ruined for the Ordinary: The Adventure of Hearing and Obeying God's Voice*
By Joy Dawson

*Passion Pursuit: what kind of love are you making?*
By Linda Dillow and Dr. Juli Slattery

*Pulling Back the Shades: Erotica, Intimacy, and the Longings of a Woman's Heart*
By Dannah Gresh and Dr. Juli Slattery

*Rid of my Disgrace: Hope and Healing for Victims of Sexual Abuse*
By Justin S. Holcomb and Lindsay A. Holcomb

*Safe People: How to Find Relationships That are Good for You and Avoid Those That Aren't*
By Dr. Henry Cloud and Dr. John Townsend

**Websites**
www.AuthenticIntimacy.com
www.MaryDemuth.com
www.PureFreedom.org
www.ShannonEthridge.com